The Civilised Alternative

The Civilised Alternative

A Pattern for Protest

Jon Wynne-Tyson

CENTAUR PRESS LTD.

First published 1972 by
Centaur Press Limited, Fontwell
Sussex and 11-14 Stanhope
Mews West, London, S.W.7

ISBN 0-900000-80-5

Printed in Great Britain by
Bristol Typesetting Co. Ltd., Bristol

To my two children and to young people everywhere, for with judgment rather than luck they may yet inherit the earth

CONTENTS

Culture is activity of thought, and receptiveness to beauty and humane feeling. Scraps of information have nothing to do with it. A merely well-informed man is the most useless bore on God's earth.

A. N. WHITEHEAD, O.M., LL.D., SC.D., F.R.S

The Aims of Education

Introduction

THIS BOOK IS BASED on one very necessary assumption, namely that there is by now a significant proportion of people, most of them young, sufficiently dissatisfied with the values and actions of society to feel impelled not merely to opt out into one or other of the negative life-styles that have become the focus of the publicity media to a by-now wearisome and predictable extent, but, seeing the opportunity, to opt in to a way of life and outlook that could give a meaning, a purpose and a pattern to protest.

There is mounting evidence that today's younger generation, being more informed and in many respects more broadly intelligent than were most of their elders at the same age, are not necessarily themselves satisfied by the more publicised styles of protest chosen by many of their contemporaries. There is every indication that more and more of them are discovering that the negative answer of retreat into obsessive drug-taking, loveless sexuality and gestures of society-rejection that nevertheless are only possible while that society exists to be used and abused, is unsatisfying, inadequate and deeply frustrating to any idealistic and creative impulse.

Not only the younger generation can see that our world is in a mess. Young or old, black or white, rich or poor, we are in no doubt about this if we are capable of seeing beyond the ends of our noses. Wars, pollution, urban neurosis, over-population, colour bars, strikes, idolatrous materialism, exploitation, inflation—you name it, we (the human race) have it.

In disgust with the society created by their elders, the instinct of the young is, and to some extent always has been, to throw over the existing institutions. The instinct of the old is to retain the basic structures but look to a shift of personalities or economic priorities to achieve better results within them. The old blame the young for protesting, complaining that they have given them every material and educational advantage, and this of course is equally as true as the counter-accusation that such a reminder is only evidence of a self-satisfied attitude that proves what a god we have made of goods. But young or old, we are frightened or bewildered or frustrated or in despair at the way the world is going.

The old are not fundamentally wiser because of their age. The young are not right just because they know what is wrong. The old do not know many of the answers, and through ignorance and fear of change they have tried to equip the young to find remedies only through those existing institutions, methods and patterns of living that patently do not supply those remedies.

The old wish the young to conform rather than to reform—to repeat the pattern and yet somehow make it better. The young feel a different pattern is needed, but the old have not equipped or encouraged them to formulate it because they have passed on to the young only the tools with which they are themselves familiar.

But while the tools will not provide the answers, possibly the very extent and effect of the mess that they have inherited will prove the spur to the young to create a different, better and so a more hopeful pattern. This is what every generation expects may happen, but never before in the West have the young been better equipped with dissatisfaction and at least a partial awareness, and never before has the crisis been so great.

The young have always been rebellious, but the dullest members of the established order must be able to perceive how fundamental and logical are many of their criticisms and viewpoints. While it is true that their unrest often takes a political form that suggests a somewhat naïve notion of social and economic realities and of human nature, there are also strong indications that their dissatisfaction with orthodoxy is not only politically destructive but also reveals a desire to seek out and examine alternative concepts that may appeal to their idealism, compassion and reason. That some have sought protest or escape through drugs and other merely sensual and dead-end preoccupations does not invalidate the dissatisfaction, though it may often have erected yet one more barrier between that dissatisfaction and the achievement of a more demanding discipline than the sense-impressions of hallucination-land and genital titillation.

> 'These people had left the commune and been driven back to leaning on the system. They seemed lost. Like people between two worlds, not knowing where they belonged. I shall never forget them coming into the room—the way they looked.'

The young people so described (discussed in Chapter Two) had dropped out further than most of their contemporaries. A much greater number have stayed 'in', though increasingly doubtful of the aims and values of the system into which they were born.

Intellectually, emotionally, spiritually, very many people in Europe and America today are partial drop-outs, but they stay within the system because they do not see an alternative. Assailed on all sides by 'isms' and 'ologies' and 'anities', each of which claims to have the answer man is looking for, we tend either to give wholehearted allegiance to one banner or label, or to reject the lot and dull our frustrations, dissatisfactions and fears by trying to keep our place in the rat-race in the vague hope that somehow it will all come out right in the end.

This book is for those who cannot be so easily persuaded to adopt such extremes. Proposing no single political, religious, social or economic system as holding the answers, the author suggests that the only remedy lies in individual re-appraisal and action, based upon an eclectic analysis and reconstruction of the needs and aims of society.

Eclecticism is presented as that 'supra-ism' that must be

adopted by the more intelligent and genuinely concerned members of the present younger generation if the suicidal trends of our materialistic, violent and sick society are to be halted and reversed. All the well-worn and partial answers, it is suggested, must be made subservient to one single system that is both practicable and, in the proper sense of that word, philosophical.

The book does not side with those critics who see all young people as deliberately adopting a selfish, irresponsible and anti-social attitude, but takes the view that they are in many cases ready and willing to pursue lines of thought and action that have been ignored or inadequately presented by their elders, whether in the home, the classroom, university, the church, or by those responsible for the media of information and entertainment.

But it must be stressed again that this book is an invitation to individual effort, not to that weakness in the human spirit that so readily leads to collective action lacking individual conviction, purpose and reform. It is an appeal for independent thought, for individual self-discipline, founded on eclectic rather than sectarian reasoning, for it is believed that nothing less can answer the social problems.

We all know—or should know—by now what we must opt out from. Far less attention has been given to what we should be striving to opt in to. It is hoped that this book will help to clarify not only what is, at heart, being protested against, but also what is (or could and should be) being agitated and worked *for*. The required pattern is likely to prove a greater and more rewarding challenge than the spectacular but less demanding gestures of negative rejection that find favour with the more glib and superficial exponents of instant answers.

Older readers might at this point be reminded that it is a truism and not just a flourishing phrase that in every era the future lies with the young. We ignore this fact at their peril and at our own, and to the detriment of all succeeding generations.

* * *

In sub-titling this short book *A Pattern for Protest*, it should be made clear at the outset that no claim is being put forward that the subjects discussed, least of all those in Section Two, have been dealt with comprehensively. Factual and statistical evidence in several of the areas discussed is available in greater detail in books by other writers; some of these works are to be found listed in the short bibliography. The immediate aim is primarily to suggest a fresh framework, a new approach, a more truly civilised behavioural pattern, and to stimulate discussion rather than to bring it to an end with definitive statements on every matter. It will be gratifying if the book is seen as something more than a manual of unorthodoxy and not merely as a hand-book for a period of transition and for effective protest, but if it succeeds only in stimulating consideration of what makes for personal fulfilment and a satisfying sense of purpose in a society wherein political and governmental ambition is cynically committed to the thesis that individual and corporate self-interest will be satisfied if technology and economic growth can be held in balance to sustain materialistic complacency, it will have served its purpose—for the young, and the young-in-mind, have long seen through the speciousness of this argument. This book is for them.

Sussex, 1972 J.W.-T.

Section One

ONE

The Need for a Supra-ism

Good ends . . . can be achieved only by the employment of appropriate means. The end cannot justify the means, for the simple and obvious reason that the means employed determine the nature of the ends produced.

ALDOUS HUXLEY : *Ends and Means*

THE FIRST DRAFT OF THIS BOOK began with the chapter that now appears in Section Two under the heading 'God's in Our Heaven . . .' The transference was made because it was felt necessary to avoid, by 'bringing in God', giving an initial impression that authorship could be attributed to yet another cleric with a roll-neck sweater hastily pulled over his dog-collar.

There need be no suspicion that the purpose of this book is to sell religion—not, at least, in the restricted, denominational meaning of that word. 'Religion' is today a very branding term, but this is because most of us use it in its narrowest sense, as synonymous with sectarianism. Lovers of labels and organisations, and those content with the limitations of a sectarian bias, may find the arguments rather hard going.

If, nevertheless, Christianity is cited more often than other religious systems, this is evidence only of the necessary assumption that the majority of the book's readers will be Europeans rather than Orientals. Where he is mentioned, there is certainly no intention to portray Jesus Christ as better, wiser or more deserving of respect for his life and ideas than are other men of principle and vision less known to the West.

For all we know—and, indeed, doubts have already been cast on the matter—the man Jesus never lived at all. But if what he has been recorded as saying makes sense, the reality of his personality is of no importance whatsoever. This may not be a palatable observation to those for whom personality is inseparable from truth and belief. It cannot be denied that personality has its uses, however, and as long as it does not eclipse or become a substitute for the principle that is being expounded, it would be foolish to damn its place in the communications game too strenuously.

In touching on the influence of the Christian church, no assumption is being made that religious organisations as we now know them can any longer provide the fundamental answers to man's social and spiritual problems. But until now the churches, for all their faults, have been virtually the only organised source of moral teaching and behavioural guidance. Where they have gone wrong therefore deserves to be examined before it is possible to trace the lines on which an alternative structure, discipline or understanding may run.

This is not to suggest that the purpose of this book is to attempt a wholesale debunking of the churches, although it may be true that virtually everything about these institutions, except those first principles which supplied mortar to the foundations, needs rigorous examination and may well be in need of rejuvenation and reorientation of so profound a nature that the present organisational form of the established church is due for almost total metamorphosis.

Whatever its failings, whatever ground it does not cover, the purpose of this book is positive, not negative. The intention is to stimulate consideration and discussion of what makes for personal fulfilment and a satisfying sense of individual purpose and direction in a world increasingly dedicated to self-interest and the hollow joys of undiluted materialism. But in a congested environment one cannot rebuild without some prior demolition.

Several years ago a now-forgotten revue on the London stage contained a sketch with the line 'What it's got to do with Jesus, Jesus only knows.' A witty number, it had been written at a time when 'satire' had not yet been so hopelessly confused with ridicule and rude noises. It took account of the fact that satire involves a reasoned anger, directed at the self-satisfied, with the aim of amendment. Satire's target was, and correctly still is, the morals and manners of society, or its lack of them, and it can be distinguished from cynicism, with which it has so often been confused, by the fact that where cynicism is merely hurtful without being constructive, being often based on distortion, satire can be recognised by the accuracy (however unpalatable) of the observation.

With that definition behind us, it is surprising, or perhaps not surprising, how often the defenders of habit accuse those with more flexible minds, and with a predilection for balance, of cynicism. Hell knows no fury like men or women who have grown accustomed to their habits of thought and are suddenly faced with the threat of self-doubt and the prospect of change. Yet it is only through entering the arena of uncertainty about our judgments and acceptances that we can come to the realisation of our own potentialities. Wyndham Lewis saw an aspect of the problem when he wrote :

> 'The faith and conviction of the philosopher imposes itself on (most people) when they come in contact with it. But when they get out of touch with this influence —which tends to attach so much *importance* to everything—they naturally pitch their tone much lower, and a fatalism or frivolity where life and death are concerned is the result.' (*The Art of Being Ruled*)

Although many of us enjoy the indulgences of self-pity and of being wronged, few of us find satisfaction in a totally honest examination of our motives, aims and way of life. It is a paradox that in an era when frankness and freedom (if that is the word) have been pushed to ludicrous lengths, the pedlars of pseudo-culture allow no limits to their conspiracy of silence over what are the real reasons for our social and spiritual ills. Drugs, unhappy childhoods, poverty, industrial unrest, the colour problem, homelessness, the pill, homosexuality, these and a hundred and one other burning topics of the day are discussed, analysed, chewed over, regurgitated, redrafted and re-presented with a predictable monotony that has reduced vast sections of the public to a glazed, square-eyed, punch-drunk state of semi-consciousness that is just slightly infused by the vague notion that all the miles of wordage and picturisation, and their own passive involvement therein, are in some way contributing to a solution. Nothing, unfortunately, could be further from the truth. Such phenomena should be seen for what they are—marginal culture, carefully tailored and edited to exclude any unwelcome demand on the reader or viewer.

That the church has failed to avert this state of things is something that many of its members are willing enough to admit. What many are less willing to perceive is why it has failed. It is ironical that the answer was known to Jesus Christ even before the Christian Church was founded, for it must be said, without intention to denigrate the good that has been done by the churches in the field of social betterment, that it was Jesus's explicit wish and instruction that moral and spiritual growth (without which the most rabid agnostic must admit the human species ceases to have any meaning or justification) should come about through self-discipline and private prayer (or desire for growth in goodness) and not through the offices and structure of institutions. The founding of an organised church was precisely what he counselled *against*. Its existence, as he would have known must be the case, has resulted in Christianity too often being supplanted by churchianity; by faith and deeds giving precedence to theology, dogma and ritual; and by greed and the desire for power eclipsing both charity and love. The miracle is that in the deeds of so many dedicated churchmen some part of the spirit of Christ Jesus should have been kept alive.

But for all the dedication of its more enlightened members, the most viable charge that can be laid against the Established Church is just that—that it is established. Settled. Fixed. Fundamentally immovable. Some of us regard as pathetic, others find infuriating, the inadequate efforts of some clerics to soften the Establishment image. Increasingly itinerant archbishops of all denominations favouring that rank have been frequently pictured falling upon each other's shoulder in the various capitals of Europe and the New World. But how many of us, by now well accustomed to the kiss-hug routines of the football field, are convinced that the outward signs of friendship and accord are evidence of an inner determination among the churches not merely to band together for security, administrative co-operation and a saving of overheads, but to plan a collaborative return to those first principles of Christianity that went to the cross with their original spokesman and have been almost totally neglected ever since?

In recent years the greatest fall-off in the power of, and respect for, the Church undoubtedly came after the 1939-1945 war. This is hardly surprising. Young men and women, in the armed services and outside them, better educated and better informed, more travelled and the legatees of an equally brutal war of only twenty-five years before, had the disillusioning opportunity of witnessing the incongruous marriage of a state and church whose unity depended, for those five war years, upon creating and sustaining the naïve belief that by combatting violence with violence, hate with hate, brutality with brutality, lies with lies, a new era would be born in which understanding, brotherhood and a determination to build a bright and better world would surely emerge.

Those who don't think now doubtless didn't think then. Those who did think (and their numbers were probably greater than their fear of not swimming with the tide suggested) could think only one thing, namely that whether or not war can ever be justified, it most certainly cannot be equated with the teaching and purpose of the alleged founder of the Christian church. Although Jesus Christ would not have admitted the parentage, the 'baby' of the church was swiftly thrown away with the bath water it had so thoroughly soiled.

For let it be remembered that in Europe, the Commonwealth and America it was not a case of one church standing shoulder to shoulder with one state to combat some evil from outer space, or even some Eastern peril of totally different cultural and religious persuasion. Rather, it was one ('Christian') church siding with equal complacency with each of the contestants. With bombs and bayonets and aeroplanes being blessed on both sides, it took no great degree of intelligence to note the sickening hypocrisy of religious leaders urging their 'teams' to decimate each other with all the impersonal brutality that a rapidly advancing technology made possible.

But one can be critical of the church very easily. It is simple prey. The majority of us can no longer believe for a moment that ritual, hymn-singing, church-maintenance and concentration on almost any part of the Bible but the Sermon on the Mount add up, even if leavened by good works and the alleviation of loneliness in the old, to a living faith. Kissing footballers can be forgiven because they score goals. Kissing clerics never get away from the sidelines.

But are we, in all this easy criticism, in any position to throw stones? For we are accusing the church, the Establishment generally, of unwillingness to change and to adapt. Of infidelity to first principles. Of blindness and indifference to priorities. These are severe charges and they are justified. But they would come better from people whose own thinking and actions were free from blame.

For just how much change and inner sincerity are most of us prepared to accept and cultivate? It is very easy to lash oneself into a state of moral indignation over the treatment of black immigrants, over the right to sexual freedom, over wars in the East, over racial discrimination, over the evils of capitalism and materialism, over wage-claims and student unrest and slum-landlords. These and many other subjects make splendid excuses for another television documentary, another protest march, another sit-in, another walk-out, and a lot of hot air in pubs and coffee bars. But how many of us, young or old, are truly, unhappily concerned over these issues—so much so that we are prepared to look into our hearts and minds and think out, deeply and sincerely, a philosophy for living and a programme for personal action that will prove our concern and enable us to contribute, as only the individual can contribute, to building a more sane and hopeful world?

For this is the crunch, surely, that it is one (and the easier) thing to join a group and protest about something, vocally or with bottles and stones. It is another (and a harder) thing to work out one's place and responsibility in the scheme of things, regardless of the comforting protection, approval and judgment-blunting environment of a group, and to act upon the decisions and realisations that one comes to.

This is not to suggest that wars, racial discrimination, political systems and so forth do not present very real problems and challenges, but rather that there is no one organisational, political or sectarian answer to such phenomena. What is being suggested is that these problems, and many others, are merely symptoms of another, far greater state of imperfection in that society of human beings that is comprised of all races and nationalities. And it is this that so few of us are prepared to realise. Or, if we do realise it, then until now few have been prepared to act upon that realisation and accept what it must mean in our lives.

For what it means is this—that in place of the multiplicity of 'isms' and 'ologies' and 'anities', to some few of which most of us tend to subscribe with blinkered fervour during some part of, or phase in, our lives, we must instead be deeply and actively concerned to make all such partial answers subservient to one single system and discipline that is both philosophical and practicable. For lack of a label that will identify such a system more clearly, let us call it Eclecticism.

Eclecticism, if we are to be precise, is 'The eclectic philosophy; the eclectic method in speculation or practice' (OED). And an eclectic is anyone who selects from various systems such opinions, principles and values as he judges to be sound and rational. Someone, in short, who, recognising an element of truth in many or all systems, creates a new and fuller system therefrom. A system to which he himself can fully and without reservations subscribe.

It is arguable that by this definition we are all eclectics from the moment of birth, and it is true that even the most apathetic and non-enquiring person must be the product of innumerable 'rubbings-off', just as the acknowledged scholar in philosophy must have been influenced by systems other than that particular 'label' under which he is recognised as being a logical positivist, a neo-platonist, a metaphysician, a moralist, a dialectical materialist, an Hegelian idealist, an empiricist or whatever.

But what sorts out the drifters and subscribers to labelled wisdom from the true eclectic is that the latter's pursuit of truth is motivated not by the desire to find security and respectability within an easily identified group, but to discover common ground between himself and all those other thinking and sincere people who have taken a level look at society and the way mankind is going and, not liking what they see, are deeply concerned to find a better pattern and a more workable system.

Can we be in any doubt, when we observe the national and international problems caused by religious and political intolerance, that there is no hope for our world until a powerful minority of such men and women has permeated the educational, political, governmental and organisational framework of society to such an extent that the life-threatening, soul-destroying and anti-social trends and habits of our so-called civilisation are reversed, destroyed or transmuted to a point where compassionately informed reason triumphs over the violence, greed and materialism that presently govern our species?

Yes, of course this is going to take time. Time and effort. But it has to come if we wish to avoid annihilation or worse. For let there be no ostrich-like self-deception about this. If men and women do not learn how to deflect the present course of our specialist-scientific, technological, violent and materialistic society, we shall so consolidate a system which even by today's standards would resemble hell on earth, that there could be no hope for the continuance of human life in any form that we could today recognise as being bearable, meaningful, hopeful or, in short, humane. That some sort of existence, based on a technologically dominated termitary wherein mind would be perpetually subservient to the machine and endless scientific experimentation, might continue for hundreds of years to come, is arguable. But so what? Should it not be our concern, here and now, to help mould the future in the light of those values and ideals that have guided the greatest minds of the past? We have to remember that only while the older values are alive, or at least recorded with some degree of approval, can the standards and ambitions of a totally materialistic society be judged. There could too easily and quickly come a point when the critical faculty and the idealistic instinct have been simply eliminated from racial consciousness by persistent mis-education.

Does this make sense, or is it more desirable to hand over the future to the banana-peeling antics of those blinkered individuals who believe (if their pursuits can often be said to be influenced by belief) that technological man will 'always find an answer'?

Such strictures must seem stronger of the technologists than those that have been directed at the orthodox church. And they are intended to be. For the world is now in more danger from its technology and the often suspect wisdom of the specialist and quasi-expert than it is from any religious system. No one who is disinclined to go along with this assertion is likely to have read this far or, indeed, to have studied much of what is now common discussion in the world's press.

And what is the criticism of this plea for eclecticism likely to be? Perhaps that its greatest danger is that it, too, will become another narrow-minded label. But this could never be so if its original definition is maintained. By definition eclecticism cannot be confined.

More understandable might be the criticism that the doctrine (one must be careful with such words!) of eclecticism is too diffuse, too broad, and it is certainly true that history has proved man's enthusiasm for associating himself with narrowly-conceived, narrowly-implemented theories, packaged in clearly recognisable organisational containers and blessed, for preference, by state and church.

But this book would not have been contemplated were it not felt that the knowledge and intelligence that is to be found in many sections of society today is such that a broad and logical concept will prove acceptable to some without the packaging and labelling that has been thought necessary to give the older notions 'mob-appeal'.

The greatest danger to eclecticism—the Supra-ism that has always been within our reach, but overlooked by all who prefer to hand over their thinking to others—is not that it can be charged with being too diffuse, but that it will (like Christianity) be killed by neglect. For its drawback lies in its very merit—that it does not seek to constrict and confine, to create prejudice and hate.

But if it makes sense, why should it be neglected? Such

is our stupidity, if the case that this book sets out falls as flat as a pancake, it will not be because eclecticism has been found wanting, but because it stands for balance, tolerance and vision and does not share with the narrower isms and ologies that blinkering and bigotry that have brought the worst ideologies the biggest followings.

For eclecticism implies criticism. It suggests that all the answers cannot be found within one ology or anity, one Thisism or Thatism. This is instantly intolerable to those who have allowed organisational and sectarian propaganda to blind them to the possibility of truth in any other system of belief.

So this book may offend. It may offend the clergyman who believes in the necessity for dogma and the promotion of ritual over thought. It may offend the professional soldier who believes that by fighting evil with evil a good result can be achieved. It may offend the technologist who believes that ever more ingenious equipment can solve the problems created by our greed and blindness to ecological fact and simple statistics. It may offend the scientist who believes that the material hypothesis only is valid. It may offend the capitalist who is sold on the glib assumptions of 'economic growth'. It may offend the party-politician whose desire for personal power and reliance on political machinery blinds him to the necessity for supra-personal, supra-party answers to a nation's problems. It may offend the orthodox physician or surgeon who can see no good in medical paths that conflict with the narrow discipline of his training. It may offend, in short, many kinds of specialist and all those who can take only a compartmental, sectional view of life and their responsibilities.

It will almost certainly offend another category of person who in his way is more dangerous and anti-life than are some of the less broad-minded (not to be confused with apathetic) professionals and specialists—the perennial optimist. Critics of 'doom-books' seize hold of words such as optimism and pessimism and use them like marbles, oblivious of their precise meaning and of the fact that neither is relevant in a situation wherein we should be concerned not with arguable intangibles and extremes, but with the concrete evidence of what man is doing to himself and to his environment. The doom boom is with us and is founded on facts, not hot air. It is not pessimism to question the wisdom of polluting another river, of encouraging people to smoke, of doubling our numbers in a handful of years, any more than it is pessimism to teach a child road safety or to observe reasonable standards of hygiene.

The 'We've never had it so good' brigade, sitting in blinkered smugness before their goggle-box with the fridge and dish-washer clunking in the kitchen, argue that those who decry materialism can afford to because they have got it. Such thin over-simplifications pervert and avoid the point. There is a world of difference between ensuring our basic needs of food, shelter, clothing and reasonable amenities, and the extreme of raping the planet we live on to produce an excess of everything including our own super-abundant species. Those in control of their doom-awareness are simply advocating balance and restraint and are trying to get across the simple fact that world population growth combined with the industrial policies of developed countries have set mankind on a course for disaster. It is the very survival of society that is at stake, not its amenities. The intention of responsible observers of these facts is not to cause offence but to prompt thought, a pattern, and action. Offence is the Pavlovian-dog reaction of those opposed—through force of habit and mental inertia—to change or effort.

In any case, this book is not written for those whom it is certain to offend. Shaw's dictum that it is impossible for an Englishman to open his mouth without making some other Englishman despise him is probably a valid truism well beyond the Scilly Isles and, our species being what it is, anti-intellectualism is always likely to be fashionable in some quarters.

As will be obvious, the suggestions being made are directed at those young enough, in mind if not only in years, to maintain a flexible and receptive attitude to ideas and values. Nor is it being suggested that in the church, politics, medicine, et cetera, there are no individuals capable of understanding the need for eclecticism and of adapting and diluting their attitudes to help create a better climate and soil in which such more liberal and non-extremist ideas and policies may grow. On the contrary, there are strong indications that in nearly every field the boundaries of enlightenment are being widened. But where the greatest hope for the spread of an eclectic approach to life lies is undoubtedly in those young and developing minds that are actively dissatisfied with the values and the nature of the society they know. For it is easier to build one's house from scratch. Converting old properties invariably leads to compromise.

If what has so far been said makes any sense, it can do no harm to ask oneself: 'Have I the moral courage—and do I accept the necessity—to examine and choose from many systems of thought and behaviour without feeling any obligation to subscribe blindly or entirely to the slogan of any particular ology, ism or anity?' In the light of the national and international problems caused by religious and political intolerance, and by technological and scientific arrogance, it is difficult to conclude that thinking people can deny the necessity. The knottier question is whether one has the guts.

Again, Shaw had a maxim for the situation when he said: 'Liberty means responsibility. That is why most men dread it.'

HABIT—AND THE ORGANISATION MAN

To see the need for eclecticism is one thing. To break with habits of thought and behaviour is quite another. Considering the amount of self-congratulation man has indulged in over his status as a free-thinking animal with the power of choice, it is astonishing to note his resistance to change.

Orthodoxy and establishment values—not all of which, it might be added, are necessarily bad because they are established; a point overlooked by some of the hotter-headed protestors—are not abstract ideas imposed upon man by an autocratic system. They are what man creates for his own discipline and slavery. Nearly all of us like to be slaves to one thing or another, and most of all to the thought and behavioural pattern that is perhaps better described as Routine. The last thing in the world that most of us want is to be jolted out of our comfortable niches.

The strength of orthodoxy, the appeal of 'party lines', lie in the fact that inflexible Thou Shalt Nots satisfy those who don't want to think for themselves. The fact that they antagonise those few who do is hardly here or there. Yet every age needs its heretics far more than it needs its party-liners, though at the time this may not be obvious, and the former need a great deal more moral courage to resist the dampening tactics of the latter.

But heresy is not the same as negative denial. True-blue, red-blooded heresy is a positive, reasoned and morally-charged reaction to over-indulgence in the status-quo—a reaction pointing a path and a destination. Any idiot can say 'Shan't!' Your genuine heretic adds 'Shall!'

The habits of animals are rooted in instinctive routines that maintain the organism during its lifetime—the routines of eating, sleeping, copulating, rearing of young, grazing or hunting, ageing and finally death in one or other of those situations that stem naturally from observance of nature's laws.

Man alone, in his less than infinite wisdom, chooses to defy and bend the laws of nature, spending an increasing proportion of his time, the higher his state of so-called civilisation, in indignant amazement at the consequences of that doubtful wisdom. That 'wisdom'—better seen as a constant and spiralling condition of non-think—has led him far beyond the natural habits of habitat and procreation and has produced a perverse and self-destructive crankiness that has created habits in homo sapiens that fly in the very face of that reasonable balance between organisms that is obvious to any impartial student of natural laws and ecological fact.

Perhaps our most perverse and engrained habits are centred on our stomachs. More is said on this later, but when one considers that comparative anatomy shows that man has the physiological equipment of animals for whom a frugivorous diet is natural, Western man's obsession with the supposed necessity and virtues of a largely carnivorous eating pattern is a truly remarkable example of his powers of self-delusion. For man lacks the short bowel, the long teeth, the retractable claws, the jaw formation, and several other physiological features shared by the carnivorous species. This is not the place to argue in depth the point that we are anatomically constructed to eat only what is natural to the frugivorous anthropoids, for the evidence is readily available to anyone in doubt. The point needing to be made is that despite the fact of our physiological structure we have chosen not only to adapt ourselves (unsuccessfully, if we take note of the many physical ills that even orthodox medicine increasingly realises are due to and exacerbated by the habit) to the food natural to the carnivorous and omnivorous species, but since the advent of scientific and technological man we have so far forgotten our origins as to rely to an ever-increasing extent upon such devitalising tampering as cooking, dyeing, preserving, freezing, processing and generally 'refining' the vast majority of the things we put into our systems several times a day.

While worrying about this particular aspect of man's conversion to habits that have no raison d'être beyond expedience and profit can all too easily turn one into a food-obsessed health-faddist, there is a more than faint absurdity about those who may still be heard labelling advocates of natural food as 'cranks'. This is the one label that they themselves have earned in full by their dietetic eccentricities, however hallowed by time they may be.

Even the growing of our food, whether vegetable or animal, is subject to endless scientific meddling and poisoning in the over-worked name of progress. Anyone who had said this a few years ago would instantly have been labelled 'crank' by the 'habit-cats'. Today 'ecology' is on every lip, but although it has acquired meaning and respectability so rapidly, there is likely to be little early change in our present suicidal habit of drenching our soils and crops in chemicals whose long-term genetic effects on the human organism are simply not known and may well prove to be the hidden method of controlling the population whose very excess has been brought about by man's tampering with the laws of nature.

This is but one, if the most obvious, example of man's tendency to drift into and then passionately defend habits that can have no justification in reason or even long-term benefit. It is a subject that is dealt with later, in a different context.

The so-far mythical inhabitant of another planet, regarding dispassionately the progress of civilisation on earth, could only conclude that the human race is a species of exceedingly inquisitive ape. Apes whose experimentation has far outstripped the development of wisdom. Apes with a sense of beauty, yes; with a creative faculty, such as seen in a Rembrandt or a Beethoven, of a high order; with a command of technical skills amazingly advanced on the banana-skinning monkey. But still, none the less, apes—childishly obsessed with the process of peeling and tasting and of creating patterns of habit beyond which they have only the most fleeting ambitions to evolve.

Many of us must have the impression that it is only very recently that these now almost too obvious facts have been given consideration. Yet the groundwork for an understanding of the sociological basis of what is perhaps man's greatest handicap to a better life has long been available to anyone concerned by the blindness of men to their own fate. In the comparatively recent past Wilfred Trotter in *Instincts of the Herd in Peace and War*, and Gustave le Bon in *The Crowd*, laid a basis on which recent observers have done little else than build a more topical structure. The change has been not in the availability of the facts, but in our greater willingness, under the pressures our myopic greed has provoked, to question the soundness of our orientation.

Had such writers as Trotter and le Bon lived a little later, however, they might well have placed greater emphasis on the effects of organisations on the lives of men and on the principles that wise individuals have laid down. For a study of history shows with a depressing repetitiveness how invariably man's tendency to build an organisation to promulgate an idea leads to the eventual corruption of that idea and to the establishment in its place of the pursuit of power as an end—and, all too often, objectives that are the precise antithesis of the principles that first stimulated the creation of that organisation. For the West, the corruption of Christianity (the simple precepts of Christ) by its metamorphosis into 'churchianity' is the most obvious example.

The old dictum of 'Power corrupts' might more accurately read 'The organisation corrupts', for as a rule power is the end product rather than something that comes into being of its own volition through determined individuality.

It is difficult to recall an instance of power, in this sense of that word, that has been established without the aid of an organisation in some form or other, even if only in the shape of a band of hired assassins.

Evil, like other inefficiencies, is embodied in organisations. The larger the organisation, the greater its capacity for, and indifference to, malpractice and injustice. A crowd of three has a greater propensity for evil and irresponsibility than has the individual. A crowd of three hundred is capable of almost anything. The evil that men do lives after them in the organisations they have helped to create.

However, we must keep our criticism of organisations in perspective. After all, what comprises an organisation? It could be defined as a group of two or more people joining forces for a common end. Even the banding together of three people to write, print and distribute leaflets banning organisations involves the creation of an organisation!

Organisation stands for united action. As long as the action is worthwhile and the members of the organisation are on guard against the hidden dangers in all corporate structures, it would be unrealistic to suggest that all sizes and forms of organisation must or can be totally abolished. *Balance* must not be damned in the name of compromise. All life is adjustment of one kind or another. Rather than trying to ban our compromises, we must control them. 'Stimulate your phagocytes' by defining your compromises!

As it is unlikely, therefore, that we shall ever manage without organisations, the most we can do is to create, through education and a heightened awareness, the realisation that there is no substitute for individual improvement and for idealistic and practical goals that are of sufficient quality to make the organisation subservient to the end and to the man—not the other way round. For an organisation to maintain integrity it must arise from, and be held together by, sincerely and deeply held values and beliefs.

No, of course this ideal state is not going to be realised tomorrow. One is taking, one *has* to take, the long-term view. But 'In the long term you are dead'. One's sympathies are entirely with the young in wanting the world and wanting it now, but somehow, someday, we have to accept that unless and until men and women can take the long view and be prepared to work, against whatever and many discouragements they may meet, for the long-term end, they will never attain that true state of civilisation it is within their power to achieve.

Many of us believe that we are already civilised, yet beneath the thin veneer of material possessions and the artistic and literary products of a handful of more enlightened minds lies a jungle whose savagery and indifference is no less merciless than it was ten thousand years ago. Today's savagery is more sophisticated, more 'push-button', more justified by twisted arguments and false ideals. If there was ever such a being as the Noble Savage, he is not living today.

The major indictment of modern man is that he contributes *knowingly* to corporate greed and cruelty and is too cowardly to take his individual stand for the higher concepts and ways of life that are perfectly comprehensible to him. Though he may be a devoted father, a man of integrity in his business and social life, and a subscriber to any number of worthy causes, his indifference to the evils that are committed in his name under the banners of Necessity and For the Common Good make him no better, in a contributory sense, than the violent criminal, the drug-pusher, the arms salesman, the psychopathic mercenary, or the pathetically brutalised girl who earns her weekly wage-packet by slitting the throats of chickens as they end their brief and unnatural span suspended from a revolving belt.

The biggest organisation of all—of which the more recognisable organisations are merely cells and offshoots—is the Violent Society. As this consists entirely of individuals it cannot be any better than the many parts that make up its whole. It is astonishing how seldom this ABC fact of life is ignored.

Yet if it is true, then neither communism nor capitalism, Buddhism nor Christianity, theology nor psychology, can create a civilisation deserving of the name. Priest or politician, philosopher or psychologist, each can make his own 'mob' no better than he is himself.

The problems of a country, much less than of the world, will never be solved or even helped by party politics or institutions, but only by better people. By a change of values, not by a change of administrators from the same stable as their predecessors. Unregenerate people can only create an unregenerate organisation and an unregenerate society. Only better people can create a better society. They do not even have to create it—it is already there.

Most of the basic truths are what the confused and corrupted term simplifications. This is one of them, and I do not apologise for it.

TWO

The Unreasonable Man

The reasonable man adapts himself to the world: the unreasonable one persists in trying to adapt the world to himself. Therefore all progress depends on the unreasonable man.

GEORGE BERNARD SHAW: *Maxims for Revolutionists*

Where there is no vision, the people perish. *Proverbs*

So FAR OUR CONCERN has been with a necessarily brief summary of mankind's predicament. Some past 'remedies' have been defined and suggestions have been made as to why these have not created a better and wiser world. The need for the positive application of a purposeful and considered eclecticism has been stressed, also the restrictive influence of habit and specialisation. The violence that man does both to himself and to others, and to his environment, has been touched upon and will be considered further.

Much of this has been evident to many, and perhaps few readers who have been patient with the argument this far have seriously rejected the main conclusions. Intellectually at any rate.

But *now* what? Let us assume that we are agreed that eclecticism is the only system than can possibly lead to a more truly civilised world. Let us assume that it can only be effective through individual effort. Let us assume that it is our individual responsibility to make that effort. How, when this praiseworthy resolution has been taken, do we go about it?

There would seem to be several initial requirements. Firstly, a personal and rigorous examination and, where necessary, rejection or revision of some of our habits of thought, combined with a sincere resolution to be ruthlessly honest about our motivations, prejudices and inclinations. Secondly, a willingness to translate theory into practice by accepting the logical consequences of overhauling our thinking processes. Thirdly, the practice itself.

It is not possible, in this one book, to examine, and to suggest alternatives or changes to, all those habits of thought and behaviour that comprise the vast gamut of mankind's way of life. It must be enough to examine a few of the more obvious behavioural and thought patterns. For those sufficiently dissatisfied with the values of the society they know, such examples will be enough to suggest a basis from which to evolve an individual pattern that satisfies each participant in the new 'involvement'. These examples comprise the second section of this book. We must now, however, be concerned less with the possible nature of those habits needing re-examination than with how their revision may effectively be achieved within the existing framework of that society from which most of us are obliged to draw our livelihood.

It is all very well when one is a student or a teenage drop-out. On the one hand parents or the state are prepared to pay for one's education. On the other, being as a rule without family or other personal responsibilities, it is neither difficult nor distasteful to reject most of the surrounding social pattern and perhaps live a bit rough while sorting out one's attitudes to society, personal relationships, and so forth. Not a few students have made the experiment of communal living, particularly in parts of the U.S.A., and this experience has not been lacking in repercussions, beneficial or otherwise, for many of those involved.

But the real test—and the one we are concerned with at this point in the development of this book—must come when the adult, consciously motivated eclectic has to decide how best he or she may merge into the current social pattern in such a way as a) to convert society to, or at least not antagonise it towards, his revised way of life, and b) not to be forced into making compromises that would invalidate, both subjectively and in the eyes of society, its ethic and purpose.

This sounds a tall order, and in the demands it may make on personal integrity, moral courage and perhaps the standards of one's material life, it may well prove to be so.

What is involved? Without over-simplifying, what is necessary is not the rejection of habit as such, but the acceptance of an alternative pattern of thought and behaviour. That pattern will also become habit, just as the change of job or house or even husband, wife or nationality can be accepted and absorbed if necessity has been matched by determination.

Given the assets of a lively and enquiring mind, it is easier for young people to accept change than it is for those of us who have dug a deep and recognisable groove and are conscious of the effects of our actions not only on ourselves but on those to whom we feel we owe a responsible concern for their material and psychological well-being. In other words, it is easier for the young and single to become revolutionaries, in whatever form, than for those already saddled with the responsibilities of family and business. This is patently obvious, no doubt, yet it is surprising how impatient and unimaginative some of the un-saddled can be with the fears and doubts of those who have become involved in the orthodox pattern of society.

If the hippy communes of the 1960s taught no other lesson, at least they proved the difficulties and the disadvantages of attempting to solve the problems of the world by totally opting out from society as it now is. Indeed, it soon became apparent that it was impossible, for any length of time, for its members to opt out in anything but an intellectual or perhaps hygienic sense. 'Il faut manger' is a powerful statement of fact for any but the higher practitioners of yoga, and tacit acknowledgement of this basic truth was sadly exemplified by the drop-outs' reliance on peddling drugs not only to their fellow-hippies, but to those who, although to some degree already dissatisfied with the existing social pattern, were still living and working within it.

This is a basic matter, surely—whether society must be changed from within, which clearly must be a gradual process, or whether it is possible to opt out and, more quickly, to establish a better, separate if parallel society on principles that will not be defiled by contact with the existing system.

It is a subject that would seem to merit the edited version of the recording of a conversation with two students that now follows. One, John, is an English university student of nineteen, studying economics, who lived for a time in a commune in California. The other, Emma, also nineteen, is at a college of education, having waived the opportunity to go to university because she felt that she wished to teach younger children. Both are perhaps above average intelligence, although Emma lays claim to no particular absorption in political affairs.

J.W.: We are agreed on the validity of the ideal. That a return to the simplicity of a life based on the back-to-first-principles philosophy of Rousseau or Thoreau, excluding the violence, artificialities and greed of so-called civilisation, would be a return to sanity, to man's essential roots, and so on. But how practicable is such a notion, do you feel, in a world that is grossly over-populated and so deeply enmeshed in the mixed blessings of an advanced technology?

John: I feel it is not, it cannot be, at this time a total answer for society as a whole. I think it has individual validity. That is to say, I think that for some people, in certain geographical and economic areas, in certain circumstances, such a way of life is possible. But I think it is at this time for a few individuals—perhaps even for a few family units —only. One has seen too clearly the virtually insuperable problems of creating, over-night as it were, a whole society that can work on these lines.

Emma: But if the individual can manage it, why not a society? This is composed of individuals, after all.

John : Perhaps because a society makes more impact. Its very structure creates problems. The communes in California were very soon spending a large part of their time defending their way of life. It became clear that they would end up either being forced to conform or by simply coming to an end.

J.W.: Because of police interference?

John : The police, yes, but also the civic authorities generally. There was often a sanitation problem. Health, too. Overcrowding and subsequent infection could be serious.

J.W.: The ills created by society could not be escaped from by opting out?

John: Well, not all of them. The totally materialistic society is really sick. It has no resistance, only health services, a welfare state, and so on. If you opt out suddenly you take your viruses and your susceptibilities with you, but you have cut yourself off from the palliatives. They might not be good palliatives, but they were all you had. An urbanised culture that exists on pills and denatured food and competitiveness and tension has got into a kind of rhythm. You take some part of that rhythm with you, bad though it is. But because your resistances have been weakened, when an infection starts you are going to need the kind of medication only available in the society you have rejected.

J.W.: Perhaps the individual drop-out, even the family unit, stands more chance of success? Even if only partially successful.

John: This could be. The hippies' life-style was quite different, yet the habit of social conformation is so strong that it is difficult to prevent the pattern seeking to repeat itself. I mean, freaking out some got the way of life they wanted, living in peace and separate from normal society. With children, even. But then it was found that they were in danger of forming and defending their own orthodoxy. One could foresee the whole pattern repeating itself, given time.

Emma: Did you feel yourself drawn to that life-style?

John: Part of me did. A lot of them were nice people. But my roots were in a non-American culture, I suppose. I was part of another group—those who were drifting from one commune to another. The straight drop-outs were another group. They were the ex-convicts, the criminals. This group was often improved by the hippy environment. They were accepted non-critically. Then there were the pushers, the peddlers. The drug-peddler is a curious neo-capitalistic, entrepreneurial character, bringing money into the commune as well as selling his products within them.

Emma: He sells drugs to the society he has rejected?

J.W.: Does this worry those drop-outs who are concerned with consistency?

John: It worries some. Others feel as they do about welfare. A lot of hippies take welfare, but they say 'The system's lousy, so if it wants to be kind to us we'll take what's going and help to destroy it.'

J.W.: I feel this is getting near the crux of the problem. From what you have said it would seem that few, if any, had a consistent philosophy in what they were doing.

John: This is so. Despite welfare, despite education, young people in the States are in deep spiritual neglect within the conforming orthodoxy. They find security in attachments. The U.S. system makes survival of the family very difficult if one doesn't conform.

J.W.: But is it realistic to assume that the system can be adapted to suit the ends of the drop-outs?

John: Probably not.

J.W.: The choice surely cannot be either capitalism *or* a consistent total opting-out?

John: This has to be admitted, I think, though not everyone wants to think through to that point.

J. W.: Have not some felt that there may be an alternative life-style—if only a temporary one, a bridging style, if you like—that is neither one hundred per cent 'Thoreau' nor one hundred per cent capitalistic and technological?

John: I think the danger here could be thought to be compromise. Some say 'We can't peacefully opt out of this society; it won't let us. If we can't live peacefully with it, or without it, perhaps the only alternative is to destroy it.' This attitude is characterised by the violent policies of the Weathermen and the Black Panthers, determined to bring the masses with them.

J.W.: And they are content to use the very violence that they —or at least some drop-outs—condemn in the society they reject?

John: This is how things have moved. The good things have dried up. The early demonstrations, for instance. Most of the young people were against Vietnam and were basically non-violent in their responses; but when demonstrators only get hit on the head and gassed, while the system continues apparently unmoved, there is a feeling of helplessness. But there have been positive aspects. Increased awareness. A change in attitude towards others. Unity. Young people have learned to be better people among each other.

J.W.: And one certainly feels that the unrest and the dissatisfaction have led to a genuine and healthy disrespect for the system, even among those who continue to see no alternative to being part of it.

John: This is so and it is hopeful.

J.W.: Earlier you mentioned people you had met who had been driven back to leaning on the system. The orthodox system, that is.

John: Yes, and this had shattered them.

J.W.: It would be interesting to know what adaptation they have made since. They had presumably, as drop-outs, to some degree or other stood for a more reasonable, a more humane life; for peace, love, tranquillity, happiness, and against evil and injustice. If so, this must have continued to mean something after they had had to drop back in, as it were.

Emma: Surely it is best to control and change society from within, by setting whatever example you feel is important.

J.W.: You are thinking of communes, or something on those lines, as a kind of clearing-house, a sort of spiritual health-farm?

Emma: It might be achieved that way, by a separate society co-existing with the greater, as it were, but I feel the impact of any reform is always greatest if it takes place within the group that needs to be reformed. I was reading about the Hunza tribe recently, and they seem to have made out very well, living to an enormous age on little but river water and apricots, but such a way of life is almost unknown to the West because they do not see it taking place within their own national boundaries. And they would probably prefer a shorter life and a super-market diet even if they did!

John: As I say, there is this strong feeling that trying to alter society from within leads to compromise; that the ends are never attained. The minorities in the States are fed up with waiting.

J.W.: That is taking a very short-term view, surely. These are the early days in any serious challenging of contemporary values. Technology and the greed it has produced have brought about a rapid deterioration in values. A return to sanity, to balance, is likely to take longer than its rejection.

Emma: Dropping out in the sense of achieving total physical separation from society changes only oneself, not society, I would have thought.

John: If every young person dropped out, society would crumble because it wouldn't renew itself.

Emma: But it has been proved that in any total sense communes are unrealistic as much as idealistic. I'm not saying something has not been learned from the attempts made to drop out of society, but the fact that consistent and total dropping out has just not been found possible surely constitutes an admission of compromise being unavoidable?

John: I think that has been seen by the more aware members, yes.

Emma: In which case, wouldn't it be better to compromise positively rather than negatively?

John: Could you clarify that a little?

Emma: Well, what I mean is that it seems very hypocritical and self-destructive to compromise in the sense of leeching on to the society you have rejected to the extent of peddling drugs to it. It is one thing to accept the benefit of medical services, even of welfare in certain circumstances, but what sort of integrity does it display to exploit for gain that very system you despise, and by marketing anything so dangerous and anti-life as drugs at that?

John: I agree with you really, though it seemed at the time—when I was in the communes—that there was a kind of logic in the way they defended that aspect of their life-style. But I'll admit I didn't go into it in much depth at the time.

J.W.: Perhaps you were so affected by the blatant imperfection in the existing orthodox system—after all, you were new to American life as well as to the hippy culture—that the relief in finding an alternative society that had dropped out in disgust or through sheer inability to keep pace inclined you to an inadequately analytical acceptance of the new pattern.

John: Probably. But a part of me still has deep sympathy with anyone wanting to cut away entirely from the surrounding orthodoxy, even if this is done in a negative and counter-exploitational manner.

J.W.: That is understandable, but if that total cutting away is found to be impossible—and you have made clear why this is so—and if, as Emma says, positive compromise is surely better than negative, anti-social compromise that irritates rather than reforms the system, have we not arrived at the point where we must accept that action against the values of society has to be taken—at least by most of us—within that society, difficult though this course must sometimes be?

John: Perhaps, so long as we are talking of minimal compromise.

J.W.: Certainly we are. That is surely the essence of the matter. Isn't this where we can look to history for examples of the sort of technique required? For centuries China, for instance, was invaded by other cultures. By and large it was her policy not to oppose these invasions by physical violence, but to absorb the new cultures that the invaders brought with them. The result? China maintained her cultural integrity—though naturally every culture evolves; none is totally static. Her compromise was minimal in that she allowed the physical penetration of the invaders, knowing that to indulge in the violence and destruction of full-scale war would be to descend to the ambitions and methods of barbarians, and to invite possible extinction. It was far wiser, surely, to counter the invaders' values with her own; to absorb and, where necessary, expel through neglect, those inferior values. For such methods to succeed, one's own values, of course, have to be culturally and spiritually the stronger. That is the test.

John: When one thinks of the leaden apathy and inertia of established administrations, it is difficult not to feel hopeless about changing them.

Emma: But I take the point that any organisation or group is only as apathetic and inert as the individuals it contains.

J.W.: That strikes me as the key fact. It must surely be true that alive, constructive and mature people must, if they keep their integrity and ideals, and are on guard against the dangers inherent in institutions, build a mature society. A consistent life must give hope of a more consistent society. What has to be fought, through proper education—that is, education in values and objectives—is man's tendency to be corrupted and rendered impotent by the infiltration of poor values, sub-cultures, and by his own laziness and inefficiency.

John: And also, I would suggest, by today's concentration on specialisation.

J.W.: Certainly. Eclecticism is the diametrical opposite of specialisation. What we are really agreeing about is that education must swing from specialisation to eclecticism. As this happens, the problems of society will be solved. I nearly added 'automatically'. But this is too easy a word. No one could pretend that the establishment of a workable counter-culture is going to be either easy or quick. What matters is that we should visualise the form it has to take. Despite the frightening aspects of the world we live in, I believe we have begun to move in this direction. I am not far into middle-age, but the awareness and determination that one finds among many young people today is incomparably greater than it was after the 1939-1945 war.

Emma: What is a bit daunting to me, as a student-teacher with recent experience of being on the receiving end of orthodox education, is the prospect of infiltrating the existing system and getting anything through to the next generation. All the State wants is for teachers to train children as cogs for industry and science. A lot of my friends at College feel this, some of them perhaps subconsciously, and I am sure it accounts for much of their apathy and discontent. What do schools do to cater for people's spiritual development—often so obviously totally neglected in the home? Absolutely nothing apart from the inevitable biblical texts that get read out in assemblies.

J.W.: I can see John agrees wholeheartedly with you there, and so do I. But surely as the spread of knowledge determines what are the real needs of science and industry, the character of the labour force required will be changed. As an example, until now the 'needs' of science have been equated with untrammelled freedom to pollute and exploit natural resources. But in the past year or two there has developed, very rapidly, a tremendous realisation of where this irresponsible greed is leading us. Already there is a substantial body of recorded observations both as to the cause and cure of our ecological predicament. The remedies prescribed may as yet be too narrow and in need of a more eclectical analysis, but the trend is there and is one of the good outcomes of the scientific mind in the broadest sense of that term. Tomorrow's teacher will not, surely, be teaching the rising generation that the world is its oyster to exploit for profit without conscience, forethought or responsibility, but rather that every one of us has an obligation, not only to ourselves but to future generations, to assess his place in the scheme of things as a vital link in an inseparable chain of natural events.

John: But there is still a limit, surely. A limit to the natural resources available. A limit to the waste that is gradually replacing the wilderness!

J.W.: Yes, of course there is a limit, and here we come to the realisation that at last one is seeing expressed in more and more books, articles, documentaries and so on—namely that neither science, technology, education nor goodwill can prevent mankind's descent to extinction or, at best, the life of a standing-room-only termitary, unless the growth of world population is halted and perhaps even substantially reduced by sane and humane methods rather than as a result of a blind inertia that allows conditions to deteriorate to such a degree that our species reaches saturation point and is decimated by one or other of the fates it is not difficult to imagine.

Emma: I agree that makes sense, although I think a lot of people feel emotionally more than rationally about restrictions of family size. But what about my point that education neglects the spiritual side of people? You seem to be suggesting that all that is required is a more rational, more planned, but equally materialistic approach to world problems. This is humanism, I suppose, but do you think it is enough?

J.W.: No, I do not think it is enough. I am not religious in the sense of accepting the limitations of any label under which I could be dubbed as this or that, but I would accept, and indeed suggest, that a proper eclecticism should and doubtless will lead to the establishment of a non-denominational set of values that would amount to a positive faith. I would say that this must add up to the same thing as a religious sense. What is so important is that those accepted values should never be brought down to, and confined by, any limiting and glib label. Unless that label be eclecticism.

John: I am not sure how you are distinguishing such eclecticism from a mere compilation of enlightened facts. From a system of knowledge.

J.W.: I think that raises a very important point and I shall try to clarify it. As briefly as possible, I suggest that eclecticism can be seen under two headings. Firstly, as a gathering together of acceptable and consistent facts to create, as you put it, a system of knowledge. This is its humanistic, its scientific aspect. But secondly, I see eclecticism as the application of those facets of knowledge that have a bearing upon our relationships with each other and with all other organisms, whether animal, vegetable or mineral. I see this as the religious aspect, the religious meaning, of eclecticism. You could interpret this, I suppose, as the suggestion that a religious attitude is consistent (possibly even synony-

mous) with a deep and broad ecological awareness. In other words, it is the behavioural aspect as distinct from (though running parallel to) the intellectual aspect. I mean to go into this in more detail in the second half of my book, for it seems to me that apart from the population problem and the necessity for an eclectic outlook, our greatest hurdle is the individual one of developing that aspect of what we may term a religious consciousness that must impose upon each one of us a self-discipline and a sense of responsibility towards each other, towards ourselves, and towards our concept of a better future society. If our educational system cannot produce such a discipline, such a target, then it is not worth the money that is being spent on it. We might just as well call it a day and go out on one last, unfettered pollutional spree and so bring to an end a species that we shall thereby have admitted and proved to be fit only for the trash-bin. But would you yourselves want this? Prince Kropotkin in a 'Letter to the Young' put it to the students of his time when he wrote:
'Ask what kind of world do you want to live in? What are you good at and want to work at to build that world? What do you need to know? Demand that your teachers teach you that.'

And with a little more depth and relevance for our times, Lewis Mumford said:
'. . . we shall have to overthrow the myth of the machine and replace it with a new myth of life, a myth based upon a richer understanding of all organic processes, a sharper insight into man's positive "rôle in changing the face of the earth"—I deliberately use the words of the great geographer, Carl Sauer—and above all a deeply religious faith in man's own capacity to transform and perfect his own self and his own institutions in co-operative relation with all the forces of nature, and above all, with his fellow men. To put all our hope in the improvement of machines is the characteristic inversion and perversion of values of the present age;

and that is the reason that our machines threaten us with extinction, since they are now in the hands of deplorably unimproved men.'

THREE

Violence, Aggression and Energy

All that we are is the result of what we have thought.

Dhammapada

CERTAINLY THE CHIEF BEHAVIOURAL problem of those 'deplorably unimproved men' is their taste for violence—a taste that technology has made it all too easy and comfortable for them to indulge in without necessarily witnessing the results. While a properly balanced eclecticism can be seen to provide all the long-term answers, including to violence, mankind is nevertheless in real danger of 'solving' its problems in the short term by the sheer excess of its perverse devotion to violence against its planet and its kind.

So while urging that we never lose sight of the necessity for the eclectic outlook, the parallel insistence has to be that our objections to violence embrace a wider spectrum. Although, reasonably conceived, eclecticism must automatically bring about this wider consciousness, so important is it that we see the limitations and dangers of a narrow concern over violence that the problem deserves constant and special attention.

The motive for all reform is, ideally, selfless and compassionate concern. While desirable in this or any other context, it is not, however, an essential prerequisite for accepting the need to reduce to the absolute minimum the practice and approval of violence in all its forms.

For there is a purely self-interested reason for developing a broader and more logical detestation of violence, needing no such labels as pacificism, and this is that the human species is itself in so much danger from the violent traditions it has inherited that it is now in fear of self-obliteration or, at best, so marked a decline in civilised standards that some of the old and (perhaps for the first time in history) a significant proportion of the young are seriously questioning whether the world we are making for ourselves is worth inheriting.

It is understandable that many young people should be feeling this, yet it is depressing how few of the old can perceive that this dissatisfaction in the young is something greater, and at heart better, than mere wilful opposition to authority and orthodoxy. It would be hopelessly unrealistic and naïve to suppose that youth is in itself the guarantee and proof of shining idealism and that everything young and rebellious must necessarily be acclaimed as deserving of unqualified sympathy and tolerance. In every group, be it of age, sex, profession or persuasion, there are the hangers-on, the bother-boys, the giggle-girls, and a whole array of sub-wits who come along for the ride and the kicks. We are not concerned with these nor with their critics. We are concerned with that nucleus whose dissatisfaction is rightly and justifiably rooted in an accurate and concerned analysis of the human condition, and we are also right to be concerned by their detractors. Why are their knockers so seemingly oblivious of the root causes of unrest? It is sometimes difficult to ignore a smugness and insensitivity that suggests a readiness to accept any change for the worse. Could it be that some of us prefer to adapt ourselves to almost any depth of technology-controlled termite life to making the effort to preserve those fundamental values that alone are what should make life worth living for a truly civilised human being?

Like most unpleasant thoughts, it is one that few observers seem inclined to deal with, and it conjures up a prospect that is best fought not by negative denial but by positive assertion of what is needed to educate ourselves into a different set of values, a different stacking of the priorities. It is a prospect that must strengthen our determination to fight ignorance with eclecticism, and violence with a more responsible and creative utilisation of human energy.

Violence is today not without its critics, yet how many who condemn such publicised examples of man's inhumanity to man as the war in Vietnam express anger or surprise at the 'common man's' lack of indignation and soul-searching when his daily ration of newsprint and TV screen presents him with yet more of the atrocities of which his species is so predominantly capable?

But should this be so surprising? If a nation's culture schools its people into acceptance and approval of varied forms of violence from the cradle to the grave, is there the slightest reason for surprise that reactions are dull and blunted when the evidence of yet one more example of brutality is flashed out between a detergent commercial and a Tom and Jerry cartoon?

For who are our real gods? Not Jesus Christ, or even Gandhi, Tolstoy, Shaw, King, Fulbright or Soper, but—aside from the Che Guevara archetypal heroes of revolutionary intellectuals—almost any beefy extrovert whose fatuous exploits in the boxing ring, in Westerns, on the battle and football fields, or wherever muscle counts for most and heart and brain count for least, are given sufficient publicity to ensure that his 'personality' is created. The symbols are equally predictable. Your he-man, your all-American male, must never be long parted from the prerequisites of his virility. The gun, the fist, the charged glass, the T-bone steak, the uniform—everything, in short, that makes him less of a man and more of a conditioned bully, is what will commend him to the mob.

This is not to tilt at the place and importance of physical expression of the energies. Recreational sports may not be productive and character forming in the Tolstoyan sense, but stripped of their commercialism and the degrading heights of competitiveness and ill-feeling that this has brought about, they have their place and do not deserve—unless rooted in cruelty or anti-social behavour—the jibes directed at them by some of the more timid intellectuals.

It is the symbols that are in greater need of being challenged; for those who accept such emblems as evidence of civilised and normal existence, the virtues are invariably military, violent and anti-life. The gods are the tin products of the current cult of the personality. The clichés are words and phrases that cloak realities, in particular such military euphemisms as 'liberation', 'free-fire zone', 'wasting' and 'search and destroy'. In the last world war it was the proud boast of the British—or of their journalists—that they could 'take it' and were willing to 'lay down their lives'. Such emotive terms disguise the obvious and unexciting fact of natural life that all species have an instinct for banding together in times of danger, regardless of whether their rôle will be to take, or impose, suffering. Under stress of war, most human beings are only too willing to join mobs led by the least responsible elements society can produce—power-ambitious politicians, apostate clergy and the professional military for whom human life is merely the currency of their 'calling'.

Irony rests in the fact that the 1939-1945 war not only bred the violence of the conflicts and civil strife that have continued ever since, but also the violence of technology and greed that is not merely raping and threatening to extinguish our planet both physically and spiritually, but has created a need for higher educational standards to ensure continued industrial and commercial in-flow. Those higher educational standards have helped to produce a generation that is seeing the violence and materialism of their society ever more clearly, though some of the background is as yet not appreciated for the simple reason that the young have no memory, while the middle-aged want no criticism of an era that all too many of them enjoyed and in which it was possible to become an instant, if soon-forgotten, hero by simply doing what everyone else was doing.

Until the gross mis-education in the worship of false gods and values, so cheaply and easily symbolised by State and commercial interests, is replaced by standards and goals more worthy of man's potentialities, there can be no hope of preventing the violence that men do to each other. Cruelty, like kindness, is indivisible. Children and men cannot safely be taught to take delight in cruelty to some living things and to abhor cruelty to others.

Despite much progressive thought in America and Britain concerning the Vietnam war, pollution, technology and other burning questions of the day, the bulk of this thinking is conspicuous for its lack of balance and perception in two important respects. Firstly, it is particular in its condemnation of violence. That is to say, it is not against violence, it is against *certain sorts* of violence; or it is against violence in certain areas, towards certain people. Secondly, it is prompted by the belief that somehow the answers will come through politically-inspired action.

Politics, like war, have never solved man's problems, and in their present form they never will. In their broadest, least corrupted and non-party sense they have their part to play, but modern politics are the science of government in the narrowest, administrative and usually party sense of that word. The social organism as a whole is outside its brief. Today's major political systems, whether capitalistic or communistic, are basically as restricted, violent and materialistic as the societies they try to administer. And this is precisely why the situation shows no sign of improvement.

The reason why progressive anti-Vietnam thinking has made so little impact is not that such thinking has been wrong in its criticisms, but that it has not been sufficiently comprehensive and logical. The picksy-choosy pacifist is a mere irritation on the belly of a nation that shares his fundamental lack of concern over violence in its widest aspects. A country's traditionalists have a certain logical right to condemn such partial criticism of their conduct of their administration because their support of the wickedness of the Vietnam war is at least logical by their own violent standards, whereas the choosy pacifist who dislikes only certain wars and certain forms of violence is guilty of philosophical drift and weakens the image of more consistent objectors to a violent system. It may be predicted that when the Vietnam conflict finally drags to a close, this will be because a violent nation has become tired of not winning and tired of losing man-power, but not because of the muddled idealism of quasi-pacifists or quasi-communists.

The year 1971 produced perhaps the most ludicrous, shameful and chilling example of a violent society's hypocrisy that has ever been given publicity. Out of many equally culpable, equally successfully conditioned citizens of the United States, the chief scapegoat for Vietnam atrocities happened to be Lieutenant William Calley, and he was brought before a military court to answer for his acts of extreme brutality to defenceless civilians in the My Lai massacre. That he was guilty of the atrocities is no more in question to a balanced observer than is the guilt of his superior officers, the Saigon generals, America's military hierarchy, and all men and women (of whatever nationality) who defend and, when it suits them, ignore violence and brutality in whatever form or location it may take place.

It was hypocrisy enough that one brain-washed killer-ape should be selected to carry the guilt of those more guilty (a guilt, let it be said again, that would never have been suggested if the Johnson administration had won the Vietnam war—the shouts of triumph would have drowned any faint cries of protest). What revealed the obscene depths of society's corruption was that President Nixon, concerned that the American uniform might be tarnished as a symbol, should foster what he and his advisers chose to interpret as a majority mood of support and sympathy for Calley, thus assuredly influencing the subsequent climate of opinion in which equally if not more guilty men were also to be 'tried'.

It is the occupational risk of a soldier that he may be killed (come to that, it is also the occupational risk of a civilian). These days it is also one of the soldier's occupational risks that he may himself kill and terrorise with such enthusiasm that his atrocities, if made known, go beyond the point acceptable to some elements of society. The risk, in addition, carries the possibility of being made a scapegoat. Racing drivers, stunt artistes and mountaineers also suffer occupational hazards, as do many of us. But the racing driver who, with a lust to kill, deliberately drives his car into a crowd of people, is unlikely to be turned into a hero, any more than a mountaineer who intentionally levers out the first boulder of an avalanche on to the village below could reasonably expect to be welcomed by the remaining inhabitants of the valley.

It would be absurd to pretend that Calley was not made a scapegoat for the equally de-civilised and callous men and women above and below him in rank and intelligence, but this in no way lessens the crime of those who have elevated a brutalised, psychopathic killer to the status of hero. By this shocking example of how a violence-worshipping society can transmute its worst evils into spurious good, the American nation has outstandingly confirmed its conviction that brutality and violence are the supreme rights. It is one more infamous milestone in human history, on a level with white behaviour in the age of colonial expansion, a period that proves all too conclusively that the spirit of My Lai has long been embedded in the nature of the Anglo-Saxons. Such episodes are to be placed at equal distance from the barbarous monuments to what the British did in India and to Dresden, what the Nazis did in Germany and Poland, what the Japanese did in the Far East, what the Communists did in Czechoslovakia, what the Star Chamber, the Mukti Bahini, the Stern Gang and Irgun Zvai Leumi terrorists and most nations and tribes and sects have done over and over again to assert the superiority of, and preference for, the obscene and degrading evil of total violence.

As forty-three per cent of the 1971 Louis Harris national survey interviewees said they themselves would obey orders to shoot old men, women and children 'suspected of aiding the enemy,' one may well wonder if we shall ever cease to need further evidence that nothing is achieved by cruelty but the sowing of the same vicious seed. We record with gloating mock-horror the brutalities in Bangla Desh where with 1,200-1,500 people to the square mile the rat-pound realities of over-population have been seen in action, but what have Indians and Pakistanis to learn from the West?

It takes the degradations of war to win the approval and sentimentality of unthinking members of a fundamentally violent society. It may have seemed tough luck on Calley, at least at the beginning of his rapid transformation from infanticidal thug to all-American, bemedalled and battle-hymn-immortalised hero, that he was the one to be brought, so briefly, to account, but the fact remains that to deny the principle that we are responsible for our actions, which is in effect what any mitigation of the sentence passed on Calley must inevitably have done, is to allow just one more win for those who want brutality to be equated with normality and respectability.

And unfortunately a huge proportion of our species wants precisely that. The cult of violence is intricately bound up with tradition, sentimentality, and that inherent or inbred cruelty that is all too apparent in so many people who favour violent responses to the problems, recreations and dietary choices of society. To such people soldiers are always 'boys', irrespective of the fact that the bulk of such emotively described men are merely trained adult murderers dressed in uniforms that make their deeds respectable within their own nation's boundaries. These are hard words, perhaps, when many of one's own friends and relatives will have done military service—with or without any particular conviction or forethought—and are ordinary and otherwise kindly and decent people.

But the fact remains that while we should recognise the professional military, politicians, armament manufacturers and all other purveyors of violence as the chief 'villains' (inasmuch as it is possible at all to pin guilt on to individuals), it is supremely dangerous to sentimentalise over either the Calley or the ordinary John Citizen end-products of a brutal system. While hatred of people gets us nowhere, and while it can only antagonise and create ill-feeling to condemn every individual who finds himself caught up in a rapacious and violent system, it is nevertheless essential that we learn to greet the bloody acts of ordinary men with disgust and contempt for the values they have absorbed rather than with misplaced and irrelevant praise for whatever incidental qualities of self-sacrifice or endurance may have been shown by individuals involved. If we acknowledge their acts with praise, any psychopathic, conditioned killer knows he has a sporting chance of getting away with —and getting medals and acclaim for—an intensification and refinement of murder and cruelty.

But the ultimate hypocrisy is the pretence that atrocity can be limited. That arming and slaughtering are necessary and beneficial so long as we periodically tidy up the rules. For the atrocity is war. Correction. The atrocity is violence. Once we accept the obscenities of cruelty, in whatever form, we must also accept the impossibility of arguing degrees. It is O.K. to hunt a hare with a pack of hounds. It is not O.K. to set one's dog on to a cat (though it *is* O.K. to torture the cat in a laboratory if a manufacturer wishes to perfect a new face powder). It is O.K. to 'waste' a 'gook' if you are in uniform. It is not O.K. to waste your wife's lover (though it might be if he was a gook too). It is O.K. to batter a gook's baby, but not your own. And so on—the nonsense could be continued indefinitely.

However, learning to live and make value judgments would be a good deal easier if we inhabited a two-tone world of black and white, for tempting as it may be to some to see all policemen as brutal 'fuzz', all members of the armed services as thugs, and all those who hunt or shoot as slavering sadists, such is the complexity of the human mind that these classes contain much the same proportion of otherwise responsible and well-meaning people as may be found in most other sections of society. The balanced observer is made continually aware of men's extraordinary facility for developing blind spots in their natures and thinking—a facility that encourages more consistent people at times to write the world off as a lunatic asylum. Dichotomy in the amoeba is acceptable because it is purposive; in man it may be tolerable and even amusing in certain situations, but at other levels it can only sadden and sicken by the evidence it provides of our willingness to abandon reason and judgment for the sub-values of a vicious and destructive nihilism. The dichotomous nature of mis-educated man is never more obvious than in times of war.

Again one returns, inexorably and without apology, to the indivisibility of cruelty. Brutalised by the indiscriminate war machine, Calley and many of his fellow-soldiers, assured of their racial superiority, were not murdering women and children in My Lai. They were merely wasting gooks and slopes. How far, at one extreme, is this from acceptance of the indifferent and unnecessary slaughter of animals for food? Their killing and maiming in the name of sport? Their abuse in the vivisection laboratories? It is a short step, surely, from our exploitation of other species to the competitive 'body-counts' of gooks in Vietnam. And how far, at the other extreme, is this callousness from the science-and-technology-controlled environment in which arrogant and emotionless men may not only be destroying and exploiting existing life forms, but will have taken it upon themselves even to create and select life and to claim the dominion of little white-coated gods over every species including their own? The eclectic who can see this has seen almost everything that needs to be seen about the ethics of violence. He can work the rest out for himself.

But while thinking on these lines he might consider one more aspect of the inconsistency of our attitudes. In a permissive, violent society we care precious little for the sanctity of life, human or animal, until, paradoxically, we reach an age when for many of us death would be a happy release. At this stage society becomes grimly determined to keep our outworn bodies and minds in a state of painful or vegetable existence until it can concede defeat with a clear conscience, its only occasional relaxation of this tyranny being a willingness to strive not too officiously to keep alive. Even those who express an unequivocal desire to be released from some protracted terminal nightmare of existence are regarded with considerably less sympathy and admiration than a keen conscript ambitious to boast of a high body-count. Whereas in life we are continually sentencing to death, on the approach of death the sentence is too often one of life. It is a further example of the state of unbalance brought about by sentiments that are related more to tradition, habit and muddle-headedness than to compassion and the facts of existence. That there are problems to be overcome in making euthanasia responsibly workable cannot be denied, but there is no reason to suppose that these are insuperable, and it is one more item on the charge-list against mankind and the inflexible traditions and institutions that have always been such a brake on true progress that even today no real advance is being made towards a more compassionate evaluation of our responsibilities towards the mounting numbers of the hopelessly sick who have had to forgo life for the frightening and often guilt-ridden shadow-play of mere existence.

But the faces of cruelty are legion. It is sadly ironic that many of today's 'drop-outs' have identified, or at least felt sympathy, with those hippy cults that have been responsible for murder and violence in American east coast communities. But a brutalised murderer is a brutalised murderer whether he is a hippy or a uniformed thug riddling Vietnam babies as though they were beer-cans. Indeed, there is no logic in pretending that there is any difference between the two, for their one great bond is that they are both perfect examples and logical products of the violent society that has given them their identity. This is not to suggest that psychopathic killers like Charles Manson are representative of all members of the hippy cult. Quite the opposite. Such a product is a total drop-*in* rather than a drop-*out*. Society has taught him its lessons all too well. If such people go to the chair or are put away for life, they are paying the penalty for being all too successfully brain-washed. Here, if anywhere, is where they could claim to have been treated unjustly.

Those who drop out of society would do so most

effectively if they were prepared and equipped to show it a better pattern. Fighting society with its own deficient weapons is to perpetuate the system that is despised, not to destroy or improve it. Violence and materialism can never be successfully fought by anything but a higher ethic, though man has been trying to prove the opposite through centuries of insensate carnage and injustice. Has he at last reached a degree of intelligence that will enable him to halt the cycle of kill and counter-kill?

Because of this long history of brutality and avarice, one of Western man's pet notions is that he is by nature and instinct aggressive. Even if he has reached the point of realising that this may not be a wholly desirable condition, possibly going so far as to admit to the *problem* of his aggressive instincts, he is still concerned with channelling those aggressions into acceptable modes of expression, not with dismissing, by proving false, the basic assumption of an innate predisposition to violence.

If the truth be told, Western man, a member of a violent society, rather prides himself on his belligerence. He does not really want to be free of his aggressions, though he has flashes of feeling that perhaps he ought to channel them into less anti-social behaviour than slaughtering Asians, bashing blacks, raping his planet, and in general behaving like nothing else on earth or in jungle has ever behaved before.

Many have been the sociological works that earnestly discuss the problems of man's aggression, and invariably the conclusion the reader is left with is that the basic premise of man's violent nature cannot be questioned.

But as with all sweeping assumptions, it is the exception that disproves the rule. Man cannot claim an instinct for aggression if many of his species show no such instinct and manage to live normal and unfrustrated lives without killing their fellows, hunting, fighting, persecuting minorities, thrashing their wives and dogs or tormenting their children. Indeed, if only one member of the human race displayed no urge to indulge in violent aggression while being in normal health, it would be enough to disprove the assumption of homo sapiens' ineradicable instinct of violence.

We are so sold on the cult of violence and on the sentiments surrounding aggression that we no longer examine the basic premise, being too taken up with studying the symptoms and shedding crocodile tears. For how we love all those carefully documented findings that agonise over the symptoms while leaving our consciences purged and guiltless because, after all, we are only doing what comes naturally. The problem, today's message runs, is to be aggressive in other directions. If there is one message that is acceptable to Western man it is that he can vary the status quo without actually changing it, for variety is indeed the spice of life to those who find nothing much basically wrong with the world as it is.

'But man is aggressive,' some will say. 'If I feel the need for violent expression, this is evidence of my instinct for violence.' Not necessarily. It is much more likely to be evidence of an upbringing within a society sold on the virtues of violence. There are always exceptions, but by and large children who are brought up by parents concerned to impart the notions of pity rather than cruelty, of gratitude rather than greed, of understanding rather than the truculent assertion of ego, turn out 'naturally' non-aggressive just as their fellows who are brought up to grab and guzzle, to compete for the sake of competing rather than to strive for the sake of attaining the highest standards in whatever task has been set, to counter force with force and hate with hate, turn out 'naturally' aggressive, rapacious and satisfied only by the exploitation of others and of their surroundings.

Clearly other factors play their part. Early insecurity can profoundly influence character and values. So, as it is being increasingly realised, can diet. 'We are what we eat', it has been said, and this is one important factor that may help to explain why Western man is so ready to claim aggression as an instinct. If we adopt the dietary pattern of the hyena we should not be surprised by hyenaish behaviour; though even the truly carnivorous species, under natural conditions, prove that their aggressions are for the purpose of obtaining their food or defending their territory and not for the insensate actions of wilfully rapacious man.

As already mentioned, although largely a meat-eater, Western man is in fact (by habit, not instinctually) omnivorous rather than carnivorous. The imagination boggles at what his behaviour would be if his diet consisted entirely of raw steak, but as he would kill himself with such a diet even sooner than he does at present, perhaps we need not fear this possibility. The historical, climatic and geographical reasons for this omnivorous pattern can be traced easily enough and need not concern us here. Our concern is more with how man is than with how he has got to be that way.

So what about the 'is-ness' of his aggression? Is man in fact as aggressive as we in the West like to make out? Or to put it another way, need and would he be if he was left alone by all those pressures that are determined to keep him that way? More of today's young than at any previous point in history would reply to this with an outright and convinced 'no!' They have seen, and have in many cases reacted against the fact, that Western man is schooled in violence and greed from the moment he is born. The society into which he arrives is incessantly concerned to persuade him of the merits of violence. From the moment that his scarcely co-ordinated fingers try to push away the 'nice beef stew' and the small gobbets of flesh that most anxious and deluded mothers try to push into his system (all those battles of the high-chair would hardly be necessary if man was naturally the carnivore that some still claim), the Western baby is learning that his society rests squarely on the credo of 'I kill, therefore I am.'

But a credo is all that it is. It is not a fact in nature.

Not for man. For the hyena, yes, but for man—who prides himself on being Top Species—there is the least possible excuse for such a claim. If anything, man's purpose is surely the precise opposite of the hyena's. The hyena is fully sold on the concept of Nature-red-in-tooth-and-claw. If man has any justification at all for standing on his hind legs and developing his mental processes, that justification is that he can see and work towards an improved pattern. Can anyone seriously argue that the violence in which man indulges so readily and on so many levels is part of such a pattern? It is a pattern that may be explained by history and seen as a remnant of the past that has outgrown whatever usefulness it may have had, but to say that it should continue to have any place in a world that has so often had to learn (or at least suffer from) the futility of violence is to admit nothing more praiseworthy or evolutionally hopeful than that we have become accustomed to our violence and do not really wish to give it up. A reasonable attitude in the hyena, but despicable and provably short-sighted in man.

One of the stumbling blocks to Western man's rejection of the cult of violence has been the portrayal by some churchmen of the character of the man Jesus. This has doubtless led to many of the disparaging dismissals of the Christian solution to violence on the grounds that its emphasis on love produces self-deception and limited results. Such critics dislike any denial of the reality of the aggressive instinct and they fear a moral and idealising approach that in their view is entirely passive, non-resistant to evil, and so likely to produce effeminacy and weakness.

Such feeble criticism would not deserve examination did it not deceive so many who are open to persuasion of the desirability of violent solutions. But nobody reading St. Mark's gospel could dismiss the figure of Jesus Christ as 'meek and mild'. If the present leaders of the Christian church had shown half his vitality, moral courage and determination to fight evil on all levels, they would now be having a far more effective say in the conduct of society.

We are back to the problem of definition. Love must not be confused with sentimentality. Love can and should mean an outgoing and active concern. As for 'aggression', this becomes a dirty word only if it stands for the self-centred assertion of one's own importance and a competitive and combative attitude towards everyone else with a ruthless lack of concern for their well-being. Such, indeed, is the basis for all that is worst in human relationships on every level. But 'aggression' can equally easily mean the energetic assertion of our 'better selves', a readiness to oppose all forms of evil, and a concerned participation in the struggle for justice for all. In this context, aggression is the active face of love.

The definitions are for us to choose. The man who allows his aggressiveness to dominate him and control his relationships is a miserable specimen of manhood. The man who acknowledges his own energy (it is the better word) and utilises it for the common good will contribute much to others and also to his own self-realisation. True manliness is not to be equated with egotism and selfishness. That is strictly for the kids, as psychologists can confirm.

The last paragraph raises a further aspect that should be considered. That word 'aggression' has that nice punchy sound that appeals to a society whose genealogical shield would most fittingly be quartered by a bomb, a fist, a rifle and a jumbo steak done rare.

But how much of the attitudinising of a violent society can be excused by the real need to be violent, and how much can be seen as the perverted use of—not violence, but energy?

Energy is not nearly such an 'in' word today as aggression, yet it is perhaps a far more accurate definition of what prompts mankind's activities and endeavour. If curiosity is the motivation, energy is the activator. The ape peeling his banana is showing an inquisitive energy. The ape swinging from branch to branch and chasing other apes just for the hell of it is showing a playful energy. The ape catching fleas, climbing from danger, eating, copulating, grooming and defending his relatives from the perils of the jungle is expressing energy in its various and necessary forms. But *energy*, not aggression. Like other species, the ape may at times have to show aggression, but this is a relatively rare obligation for the frugivorous species.

Need the parallel with man, so-called super-ape (though with many more acquired hyena characteristics), be laboured too hard? How many of his activities could more reasonably, less sensationally, be seen simply as outlets for energy? Do we need to cherish and promote this big illusion that man is a constantly pent-up bundle of violent aggressions that must be unleashed left, right and centre every day in every possible way if he is not to suffer from repression and inhibition? If the answer is 'no' it is more likely to come from the mouths of the professional military, their colleagues in armaments, and from politicians and certain one-track psychologists, than from anyone who has taken the eclectic view of man's behaviour and inclinations.

In our attempts to explain and justify our violence and brutality—that bad behavioural pattern we now take for our natural state of being—specialists and experts in this and that are fully stretched in the ludicrous pursuit of fresh analyses of, and palliatives for, a condition from which we need not be suffering and that we have brought upon ourselves entirely by our cupidity, over-sophistication and materialistic short-sightedness. Putting it into crisper shape, our wisdom is way behind our knowledge. We have monkeyed into almost everything we have come across, dissecting, analysing and destroying whatever has lain in our path, and half the time without even the justification that we were thereby trying to bring about any improvement. If man deserves an epitaph, it might be that he was the biggest banana-peeler of all time. Just how much of it has been energy wrongly directed? Energy in isolation, uninformed by that wisdom that can come only from the quieter centre of man's being—from the philosophies that have been the result of contemplation and observance and of an awareness of the unquestionable necessity for a sense of direction based on ethical (as distinct from expedient) principles, and that are today impatiently ignored as being irrelevant to the pushing, grasping ambitions of technological man, so arrogantly and smugly certain that his monkey-made machines will somehow provide all the answers.

Poor hyena-apes, our time for Re-think is running out fast!

Section Two

The first section of this book has been concerned mainly with the current predicament of society and with suggesting that the solution lies in a revised pattern of thought and behaviour based on an eclectic and responsible involvement by every individual who accepts that specialisation and organisational activity must be subordinate to personal excellence.
Some emphasis has been laid on the realisation that the mutually inclusive problems of pollution and population comprise the biggest material challenge the world has ever known, but that in learning to live by the laws of nature if he is not to perish by flouting them, man must above all temper his technological blindness and scientific arrogance by a deeper humility, a wider awareness, a greater compassion. Although self-interest is natural to all species, if man is guided exclusively by short-term personal advantage and his grossly unbalanced addiction to violence, he will inherit long-term extinction—or worse.
The following chapters discuss, in the light of this argument, some of those habits of thought and behaviour that need to be reviewed and revised. Some of the matters raised are orthodoxies that are already being questioned. Others break ground to which orthodoxy is still in general opposed. All are put forward as relevant arguments that it is hoped may lead to further discussion and, above all, action on the part of any person, young or old, who is concerned with the way the world is going.

FOUR

Red in Tooth and Claw

To a man whose mind is free there is something even more intolerable in the suffering of animals than in the sufferings of men. For with the latter it is at least admitted that suffering is evil and that the man who causes it is a criminal. But thousands of animals are uselessly butchered every day without a shadow of remorse. If any man were to refer to it, he would be thought ridiculous. And that is the unpardonable crime. That alone is the justification of all that men may suffer. It cries vengeance upon all the human race. If God exists and tolerates it, it cries vengeance upon God. If there exists a good God, even the most humble of living things must be saved. If God is good only to the strong, if there is no justice for the weak and lowly, for the poor creatures who are offered up as a sacrifice to humanity, then there is no such thing as goodness, no such thing as justice . . .

ROMAIN ROLLAND : *Jean Christophe*

Nowhere in nature is there the slightest evidence of kindness, of consideration, or a feeling for the suffering and the weak, except in the narrow circle of brief family life. Man furnishes no exception to the rule. He seems to add the treachery and deceit that the other animals in the main do not practise, to all the other cruelties that move his life.

CLARENCE DARROW

The unpardonable forgetfulness in which the lower animals have hitherto been left by the moralists of Europe is well known. It is pretended that the beasts have no rights. They persuade themselves that our conduct in regard to them has nothing to do with morals or (to speak the language of their morality) that we have no duties towards animals; a doctrine revolting, gross, and barbarous . . .

SCHOPENHAUER

The Civilised Alternative

Man, in order to be the highest of all the series of living beings, is in that proportion bound to prove his right to the supreme place and power and his asserted claims to moral and mental superiority, by his conduct. In brief, in so far only as he proves himself to be the beneficent ruler and pacificator, and not the selfish tyrant of the world, can he have any just title to moral pre-eminence.

HOWARD WILLIAMS, M.A.: *The Ethics of Diet*

It was first of all necessary to civilise man in relation to his fellow men. That task is already well-advanced and makes progress daily. But it is also necessary to civilise man in relation to nature. There, everything remains to be done . . . Philosophy has concerned itself but little with man beyond man, and has examined only superficially, almost with a smile of disdain, man's relationship with things, and with animals, which in his eyes are merely things. But are there not depths here for the thinker? Must one suppose oneself mad because one has the sentiment of universal pity in one's heart? Are there not certain laws of mysterious equity that pertain to the whole sum of things, and that are transgressed by the thoughtless, useless behaviour of man to animals? . . . For myself, I believe that pity is a law like justice, and that kindness is a duty like uprightness. That which is weak has the right to the kindness and pity of that which is strong. Animals are weak because they are less intelligent. Let us therefore be kind and compassionate towards them. In the relations of man with the animals, with the flowers, with all the objects of creation, there is a whole great ethic [*toute une grande morale*] scarcely seen as yet, but which will eventually break through into the light and be the corollary and the complement to human ethics.

VICTOR HUGO

As AN EXAMINATION of violence ended the first section of this book, and since violence creates such a large proportion of man's problems of adjustment to that civilised way of life that is within his intellectual grasp but, so far, beyond his general ambition, the second section may fittingly open with the same problem.

The same problem, but a different facet. It has already been said, and can hardly seriously be disputed, that cruelty is indivisible. If this is accepted, the implications demand a reassessment of a tremendous range of human activity.

We are agreed, no doubt, that to deserve the adjective 'civilised' man must be concerned about the violence that he is willing to inflict upon his own species. Many men do already have this concern. That their violence towards each other is still so widespread is no defence of violence, but merely evidence of man's reluctance to examine and reject his patterns of behaviour.

But if the violence in cruelty is indivisible, and if it is illogical to deplore the violence of the thug who will mow down women and children and is then brought before a military court in a uniform whose ribbons testify to our approval of his prowess in slaughtering their husbands and fathers, then a rational man must accept that it is equally illogical to suggest that we should condemn cruelty to our own kind and condone it when directed at other species.

The thinking behind this suggestion is hardly new. Many of the greatest minds of the past have abhorred man's brutal exploitation of animals. Even a very short selection will include Apollonius, Asoka, Blake, Buddha, Clement,

Darwin, da Vinci, Diogenes, Einstein, Milton, Newton, Ovid, Origen, Plato, Plotinus, Pythagoras, Plutarch, Pope, Rousseau, Swedenborg, Shelley, Socrates, Shaw, Thoreau, Tolstoy, Voltaire, Wesley, Wagner and Zoroaster. A comparable list of modern names would fill many pages and would include people eminent in the arts, science, medicine, fashion, sport, commerce, and even the armed services—for whatever criticism of the military mentality this book may contain, it should be noted that it is often those who have been most involved with violence who have reacted most strongly against it.

But not only is man illogical to ignore the inconsistency of his cruelty, he is extremely stupid and short-sighted. His violence has played the major rôle in his dominion over other animals. Now this very violence has been seen as a threat to man's survival, and he cannot any longer imagine that he can achieve a successful synthesis while continuing to subscribe to such a divided ethic.

'Yes, but,' the cry will come from the stomach-dominated majority of Westerners whose memory of breakfast's bacon is clouded only by anticipation of dinner's chicken, 'we must first eliminate the cruelty of men towards men, and *then* we can start to worry about the animals.' 'Then' has always been a useful little word and in such contexts is invariably and comfortingly well beyond the life span of its user.

But while there is no difficulty in understanding why the majority of us allow our lives to be governed by the motto of the Grand Duchy of Luxembourg ('We want to stay as we are'), such reasoning is simply not good enough at a time when the consequences of our dishonest and muddled thinking are catching up with us so fast. In our own interests, if not in those of other species, we have got to get ourselves sorted out.

Cruelty is indivisible not only in its outward effects but also in the spiritual and mental damage it does to the man or woman who is attempting to live on two opposed levels. From cot to grave we are all being educated, for better or for worse, and it is arrant nonsense to suggest that a child who, say, is brought up to course hares and reverence the depraved philosophy of a Nietzsche, or a Hemingway, will develop an outlook and character that has not been tainted by the devolutionary values of such caricatures of the civilised man.

When the need for the eradication of cruelty is truly accepted, there can be no argument as to which brutality should be eliminated first. Cruelty is cruelty. When convinced of this, the John Citizen who ceases to beat his wife and children will within the shortest possible time also lose any enjoyment of or excuse for whatever other sadistic pursuits, or merely thoughtless patterns of habit, mis-education and apathy have bred into him.

Man was the first killer ape and, one devoutly hopes, the last. Much of his education at present consists in learning what forms of aggression are socially acceptable and what are not. If he is to survive, his choice of outlets for the indulgence of violence (or mis-directed energy) must be enormously reduced. It cannot be over-emphasised that the violence of cruelty is indivisible, or that it is just as necessary for man to curb his brutality towards animals as towards his own species. There is a world of difference between a compassionate nature and a temperament that selects the targets for its cruelty. Neither the cruel nor the compassionate man is likely to be wholly consistent, any more than are the Jains of India whose need to draw breath, even though through butter-muslin, must necessarily contribute to that chain of birth and death that binds all material life in involuntary slavery to a pattern whose purpose only men are capable of questioning. But awareness of the necessity for consistency, and a constant striving to perfect that consistency, would help to win a great part of the battle for survival bloodlessly.

Such realisations are not lost on the Eclectic. He will recognise them as just as obviously true and logical as is the necessity to reduce pollution, eliminate slums, deplore racial intolerance, conserve natural resources and control the upward spiral of population. Unfortunately it is the Specialist rather than the Eclectic who needs to broaden his horizon.

Even so forceful and clear a writer as Paul Ehrlich has proved his inability to reject the baneful influence of the culture in which he has been brought up. For all his considerable qualities as an ecologist, as a product of a materialistic and violent society he still subscribes to a *desidero* rather than to a *credo,* and this is somewhat startlingly revealed in his list of mankind's Inalienable Rights (*vide The Population Bomb*):

1. The right to limit our families.
2. The right to eat.
3. The right to eat meat.
4. The right to drink pure water.
5. The right to live uncrowded.
6. The right to avoid regimentation.
7. The right to hunt and fish.
8. The right to view natural beauty.
9. The right to breathe clean air.
10. The right to silence.
11. The right to avoid pesticide poisoning.
12. The right to be free of thermo-nuclear war.
13. The right to educate our children.
14. The right to have grandchildren.
15. The right to have great-grandchildren.

The right to eat meat, to hunt and to fish! Ignoring whether Dr. Ehrlich's twelfth desideratum proves a fuddy-duddy nostalgia for cold steel and the thin red line, and putting aside the question of who or what conferred upon man any such 'rights' as these, the third and seventh being unnecessary and unnatural to the terminal form of *hominoidea* (i.e., us), one must gravely chide the worthy doctor for making assertions that fly directly in the face of the first principles of ecology.

Ecology is essentially a matter of balance—the balance

between all living organisms. Man's predatory greed and his cultivation of habits that are unnatural to his chemistry have done more to upset the ecological balance than any other single factor in the evolution of this planet, and a prime example of his crass insensitivity to this balance, second only to the excessive number of his own species, has been his exploitation of animals for food and sport. Stock-farming must take enormous responsibility for the unbalancing of nature, yet not content with the damage he has done on land and in the air, man's latest proposal has been to tamper with the largely invisible and unknown ecology of the last remaining and largest area on earth—the sea around us.

Leaving Dr. Ehrlich shame-facedly editing down his fifteen commandments to twelve or even ten (which is of course to make the arrogant assumption that he will not write off the whole of this book as the product of a nut), let us consider for a moment the carefully forgotten fact that even today flesh-eating humans are in a minority. Were this not so, the world population could not be as large as it is, for cattle need about eight times more land for food and rearing than do human beings, while only a small proportion of the food they eat comes back to us in the form of nutrition.

If this extremely uneconomic way of obtaining food had been adopted by all nations, the land resources of the world would long since have been exhausted. Most of the fertile land devoted to cattle, which eat cereals, root and green crops and various seeds for improved milk production, could show a much quicker and more economical return if used for crops suitable for direct feeding to human beings. Ten times more cereals, weight for weight, can be grown in the same time than meat, and up to a hundred times more vegetables. Nor are we just beginning to discover these facts. A good many years ago Sir John Russell, F.R.S., estimated that 1.63 acres are necessary to support a man living on a mixed diet, whereas only .5 or .6 acres are required for a varied vegetarian diet. Of the 1.63 acres serving a meat-eater, 1.3 acres are needed solely to provide flesh foods. As a single instance of the folly of what is going on, each year we take from India, a land always verging on famine, 190,000 tons of oilseed protein to feed battery farm animals. Yet an ounce of protein a day could make all the difference between life and death to a starving child. A thought that does not unduly worry those who insist upon eating meat.

Once the mind-broadening process of eclecticism has begun, it is difficult not to feel deep anger over such realisations. One also becomes conscious of the irony and the hypocrisy (much of it initially innocent) in the attitudes of so many men and women who choose limited roles for their indignation and social consciousness. The exhortations of those who condemn society for its indifference to the plight of the starving millions (the anticipated total for the coming year is around 20 million, and as man continues to destroy the life support systems of his planet the graph will rise) would sound a lot better coming from people prepared to face, by deeds rather than words, the fact that everyone in the world could have adequate food if the enormously wasteful habit of eating meat and its by-products was sacrificed by the richer minority of the earth's inhabitants who insist upon this totally unnecessary and unnatural diet. It is deeply inconsistent to bewail poverty and starvation while continuing to consume products that ensure that vast populations must remain under-nourished. The only *eco*-logical next step for truly concerned observers of the world's predicament is to cease to consume meat and other animal products. An unpalatable fact to many—even to the conventional vegetarian who compromises his principles by eating dairy products—but one that must become progressively more inescapable.

On this score alone it is surprising that so eminent an ecologist as Dr. Ehrlich can list greed and cruelty among man's inalienable rights, but the fact that he has done so lends all the more weight to the contention that specialisation, with its blinkering and narrowing effects on mental development, must give way to eclecticism if man is ever to stand outside and above himself and see the world and his responsibility therein as a logical and purposeful whole.

It is not enough that the cleverest among us should be content with a position among the top ants in our society. It is essential that there be at least a convinced minority whose influence will significantly control the corporate spiritual direction of the termitary. (Influence, let it be noted, not power. Risking simplification, it can be said that the concerned seek influence whereas the corrupt pursue power.) In days gone by we had the idea that this was the rôle of God. Since we have successfully done away with God, we must appoint, or at least not obstruct, those qualified, however inadequately in our present state of growth, in omniscience. They are unlikely to be found in the ranks of the specialists and self-styled experts. Party-politicians and other power-seekers are disqualified by definition. As such exclusions clearly eliminate a large proportion of the human race, the problem is obviously a formidable one. But this is to digress, though perhaps with some justification if it encourages acceptance of the assertion that it is man's cruelty, ambition and specialisation that are at the root of his loveless and exploitative attitude to all living things, human and animal, and which therefore make him his own worst enemy.

As can readily be seen, the comparatively new study of ecology, with its enormously important bearing upon the whole future of this planet, is intricately involved with the vast field of mankind's eating habits. The day is gone when any of us can assume that whether we shall eat animal or vegetable products, and work to spread our eating habits into any other promising markets, are matters merely of choice and enterprise. We now know, and none more clearly than those scientists and specialists who work on these lines, that even if a world programme for the control of population were put into operation as from next month on, there is simply not the terrestrial space available to permit any wide further spread of the minority luxury habit of consuming dead animals.

So where the old-style vegetarian produced evidence (and plenty is available) to support ethical, aesthetic, anatomical and medical objections to meat-eating, today's diet-reformer (if for less idealistic reasons) is facing the same necessity to question the hallowed rôle of cooked flesh and may be found in the laboratories and writing reports and articles for publication in farming journals, technical and agricultural publications, and increasingly in the columns of the world press which is as yet in the early stages of realising just what it is all adding up to.

For what it is all adding up to is that man's attitude to other living organisms is being changed by a combination of different states of awareness. Firstly, man is becoming better educated. Or if the phrasing of that sentence might be questioned by some, at least he now has access to more information. Secondly, the general trend of his cruelty is away from direct, eyeball to eyeball violence against those he wishes to exploit or decimate. There are exceptions to this statement, certainly, but on balance the evidence supports it. Thirdly, the many facets of the science of ecology are teaching him the dangers in greed, violence, the unbalancing of nature, and habits of life that are foreign to his physiology. Fourthly, and this applies particularly to the younger generation in the Western world, there has been a significant revulsion from the extreme violence and materialism that has come to a head after two world wars and an almost uncountable number of lesser but equally brutal conflicts. It is a revulsion that may not as yet have extended very far towards species other than mankind, but the signs are present and are hopeful, and it would be unreasonable to suppose that the wider awareness which is the essential prerequisite for a practical eclecticism will not encompass and get into correct perspective so enormous a field of responsibility as is indicated by the eating habits of the human race.

Because of the realisations that are beginning to flood in on us, many of the die-hards, reluctant to admit that we are in the gravest danger of so unbalancing the resources of the natural world that our very existence is seriously threatened, can be heard denying that things are as bad as they have been painted, and the more extreme (if that term can be applied to myopic conventionality) would, it seems, almost rather be found dead than submit to the demands of a rapidly growing ecological awareness.

Such advocates of the status quo might even, unconsciously, be promoting the best answer of all, for the decimation and disappearance of the human race would bring tears to few but the last remnants of homo sapiens. It has been said that if the animal kingdom had to imagine the Devil, it would have thought of Man, and for all that nature is red in tooth and claw there can have been no parallel in the natural world, prior to the advent of our species, to the indefensible field of torture and pitiless exploitation that has existed since that first aberrant ape got it into his head that he could boss the whole outfit.

No one in his senses is going to suggest that there can be any going back to the carefree, tree-swinging days when the major decisions concerned a choice of branches; whether it would be berries or a banana for breakfast; and when a nut was a nut and not some breakaway think-box tearing himself to shreds over whether his species should choose this or that destiny, or even if it had one at all.

Somewhere, one cannot help thinking, there is a middle path between the idealistic (but perhaps unrealistic—at least in the short term) retrogressions of men such as Thoreau, Rousseau, Voltaire and Alcott who saw no answer but a return to nature with the fruits of the earth in plenty for a select few, and the technology-blinded, man-must-progress enthusiast who envisages an extended universe as a solution to (or an escape from?) our problems on earth. For technology cannot just be buried under the carpet, however strongly some of us may at times feel this would be the best solution. Technology has produced good as well as evil, and while the evil that it has done to man's spirit and ambitions is greater than the destruction wrought by some of its more tangible products on the physical environment, including our own species, our challenge is clearly to learn to control our technology instead of letting it control us.

The evidence, or at least the hope, for the possibility of a middle-path answer lies in man's one inestimably valuable, if still rare and under-exercised, faculty—that of being capable of consciously reacting against those very instincts that cynics and the out-and-out materialist would have us believe he cannot shed.

To take a relatively minor instance of this, it is the contention of those who kill in the name of sport that man is 'naturally' a hunter. We tend to accept this kind of assertion in much the same way as we accept so many of the habits which it seems have been with us for ever, but which in fact may in many cases not even have been practised for as long as the absurdly brief period of man's existence in a 'sapient' state.

Contrary to the wishful thinking of those who shoot, hunt and fish, probably vast numbers of people possess no instinctive urge to kill anything whatsoever. The fact that whole populations employ armies of slaughtermen and butchers to supply them with scarcely recognisable parts of other species to be further disguised and made palatable by cooking and other processes before being lowered into their unsuitably long bowels, is no more evidence that man is naturally a meat-eater than is the idea that a child that is trained from an early age to use a gun and deaden its sensitivity to the infliction of suffering on other species is naturally a hunter.

The truth is, as most parents can testify, that the majority of children dislike, in their early life, the taste and maybe the texture of meat, and by the time they are old enough to participate in the so-called blood sports they tend to react 'instinctively' (?) against the cruelty implicit in and inseparable from killing harmless birds and animals for 'fun'. Unless, that is, they have been brought up to admire and emulate those who take their pleasures in so dismal a fashion.

'Instinct' is probably one of the most mis-used words in any language. It protects the sadist and the insensitive from criticism, justifies the actions of those politicians, industrialists and professional military who combine to keep some part or other of the world in a constant state of war or fear of war, and gives carte blanche to all who would seek to persuade us that the incessant indulgence of our least excusable senses is not only our birthright but is absolutely essential for our psychological well-being.

It is curious how the word 'instinctive' is so often used in tones of reverence that are nowadays scarcely ever discernible in talk about morality, compassion or even God. If there is one thing that is sacred to Western, materialistic man it is his right to indulge his most animalistic and least truly man-like qualities.

We are back again to the problem of taking a middle path through the extremes that so many of us prefer to the seemingly duller answers that lie in moderation and balance. What is the moderate definition of Instinct?

Clearly even modern technological urban man is still instinctive in some respects. But though his natural instincts may reasonably include the basic urges to eat, sleep, copulate, rest and breed children, these tendencies should not be confused with what might better be distinguished as *reactions* that have been bred in him due to environmental and social change rather than to his innate biological make-up.

For instance, as has already been touched upon it is the acquired 'instinct' of the global minority of our species to eat meat. With the change of climate and his geographical location, man (or some men), it has been suggested, developed the habit of eating meat, perhaps during the ice-age when vegetation became less plentiful and the protein-bearing nuts and berries were in shorter supply. The habit has continued and become blessed with the label of instinct. Yet it is no more a natural (as distinct from an introduced) instinct than is urban man's present—if sometimes inadequately developed—instinct to look both ways before crossing a busy road. It is a habit he has got into. It would be foolish and grossly unscientific to dignify it with anything more than that.

On page 100 reference was made to the fact that today's examiners of our traditional eating habits include scientists and technicians, many of whom are doubtless of a generation for whom 'crank' is the only epithet fit for those who seek to reject mankind's unnatural but time-hallowed practices for any reason other than expedience and the pressures of economic necessity. But whatever their motives, as the population increases and more land is sacrificed to housing and recreation, it is now virtually certain that it is scientists and technicians who will ensure that the habit of eating meat will increasingly be replaced by the consumption of those proteins of direct vegetable origin (some remarkably imitative of meat and currently known as TVP, or textured vegetable protein) that are already being marketed successfully all over the world, including in Britain and America, and have clearly a great future in countries whose populations have most seriously outstripped the natural or importable resources. There can be little doubt that the habit of eating vegetable proteins will become just an engrained as has the far less natural one of eating animals. Necessity breeds habit as surely as usage creates tradition.

This prospect may fill the meat-and-two-veg. school with horror and despondency, and already a number of dinosaurs have written to newspaper editors deploring this assumed threat to the future of haute cuisine. What is going to win, however, is not the plethoric wails of outraged gourmands, but the rumbling bellies of hungry children. True, given the choice and a full stomach, most children would favour neither meat nor its laboratory analogue, and there is, indeed, a large element of absurdity, explained only by man's enslavement to habit, in the idea of going to such pains to imitate something that is unnatural to our species in the first place. But if nourishing and cheaper protein can be produced in the form of synthetic meat, no starving child is likely to go along with the jeers and complaints of selfish diehards.

Certainly, as has been said, there is something absurd

about meat analogues, though the deeper joke is that would-be carnivores, in attacking the imitation, are defending an original to which they are cranks to have laid claim in the first place. The situation would have amused a Greek dramatist. But when one has got all the laughs out of one's system about 'plastic' T-bone steaks, what after all does it matter to the consumer if he is eating something that has been produced direct from the source of the protein instead of via the expensive and wasteful medium of a grazing animal? Cheap high-protein food is cheap high-protein food, and that is a fact of life that the world cannot afford to ignore. If it can be obtained without subjecting countless millions of sentient creatures to the fear and pain of the many processes, of which slaughter is only one, in the long chain of events that leads up to the appearance of a piece of charred, partially decomposed and (with the advent of the obscenities of 'factory-farming') increasingly unpalatable corpse, how can anyone but the grossly insensitive and selfish man or woman put forward a single sound objection?

Even the vested interests cannot seriously dispute the trend, for like the fur trade, whaling, shooting and hunting, stock-farming and butchery can be phased out of existence just as can any other obsolete and primitive practice. No one can hope or suggest that such a phasing-out will occur over-night, but it is a process that has already started and is entirely to be welcomed by anyone concerned to prove that man is an evolving species and not just a short-sighted and pitiless savage.

Savagery? Such a charge may seem ridiculous when one pictures mild Mr. Smith next door, or dear old Aunty Jane and her pussycats, but these mind pictures we have of ourselves are the red herrings that habit and sentiment create to disguise the brutality that lies below the thin patina of our mis-called civilisation. If in doubt about this, think about it again towards the end of the year as Christmas approaches. Christmas, that time for killing when the blood-letting has been stepped up to maximum and the Church plays with the idea of the Prince of Peace and compassion. For those who can see beyond the Belsen-like rows of dead creatures viscerated and stuffed into polythene bags, and who can imagine the extra agony and needless expenditure of sentient life, it is a time when dismay has in a few hearts at least led to a revision of values and a reassessment of one's contribution to the world whose future lies so uneasily in our sanguinary hands.

Defenders of anything, once driven into a corner, tend to conclude that the best form of defence is attack, and at this point in the development of a theme such as this one would not be surprised to hear mutters of 'What about battered babies? What about the colour problem? What about Vietnam?' For these are some of the stock retorts of those who do not want to be reminded of the diversity of man's cruelty. They are the answers of those who see, in any broad and balanced concern over mankind's greed and violence, a threat to their habits of eating, fashion or sport.

Red in Tooth and Claw

If, as has often been suggested, more people—in Britain, at least—are worried about animals than about battered babies, this is because cruelty to animals is more apparent and certainly infinitely more widespread. But it is not, in fact, even a true suggestion. We, the British, are a nation of animal sentimentalists, but this is a very different thing from being 'lovers' of animals in the sense of having any real concern for their welfare. The woman standing at the rails in her mink coat, her stomach digesting its daily quota of veal, chicken or lamb, watching her two-year-old colt break its neck or a fetlock in response to the goading of its jockey, is not really to be numbered among the nation's animal lovers, any more than are those who encourage the breeding and marketing of household pets and vie with their neighbours in owning ever larger dogs which, when they discover the cost of feeding them on tins of meat that contain a proportion of other people's ex-pets, are abandoned on some by-pass. Anyone who is interested in determining the extent of the 'animal-loving' public has only to talk to a practising veterinary surgeon. It is an experience that is hardly less sobering than enjoying the confidence of a dedicated vivisectionist.

The total area of man's cruelty to other animal species is so vast that it is possible to touch on only a few more obvious aspects, and the last sentence is a reminder that there is one practice that is on so huge and rising a scale that it demands prominent concern.

Countless millions of creatures enter the vivisection laboratories every year, many of them being subjected to the furthest extremes of suffering, often in repetitive experiments adding nothing whatsoever to medical or industrial knowledge and perfectly capable of being recorded in print and on film for use by later students and researchers.

To give some idea of vivisectional practice in the 1960s, the Federal Government of the U.S.A. allocated some 1,000 million dollars a year of the tax payers' money to biochemical research, most of this involving experimental use of animals. Some 200,000 people were engaged in this work full time, and 300 million laboratory animals were currently in use, ten dying every second.

But these are mere statistics to those bereft of imaginative concern over mankind's responsibilities to the weak and defenceless species we will buy, steal and breed for our questionable paths to knowledge. Published documentary evidence of the extent and nature of many of the hideously cruel experiments that are carried out on monkeys, dogs, cats, rodents, et cetera, is available to anyone needing proof of the purely humane argument against vivisection. But as there is always a section of orthodoxy, in whatever field of research, that holds that anything is justified if done for the benefit of mankind, it is probably less profitable to argue degrees and comparisons of suffering and cruelty than it is to examine the basic ethic by which all brutality and exploitation stands or falls.

For the case against vivisection is the same as that against war and all other forms of cruelty—that violence does not produce long-term solutions. Sometimes it may seem to do so on superficial examination, but a wrongly-contrived 'solution' must inescapably have been infected and devitiated by the degree of evil or moral sickness that went into it. There is no such thing as an evil to end evils any more than there is a war to end wars. The rule of dragons' teeth cannot be side-stepped.

This, one might say, is a natural law, and if one has recognised its validity one cannot claim or hope for any exception for the medical profession. Indeed, medicine must be particularly vulnerable to this law, for what is so especially regrettable about its reliance upon vivisectional research is that the quality of mercy is, or should be, the very basis of medical practice. Someone somewhere along the line said that people cannot serve two masters, and it is surely only a matter of common sense that any attempt to relieve suffering by inflicting it must be weakened by the harm done to the character and outlook of those who accept the necessity to seek good ends by evil means. 'Nothing,' wrote John Galsworthy, 'so endangers the fineness of the human heart as the possession of power over others; nothing so corrodes it as the callous or cruel exercise of that power; and the more helpless the creature over whom the power is cruelly or callously exercised, the more the human heart is corroded. It is recognition of this truth which has brought the conscience of our age, and with it the law, to say that we cannot any longer with impunity regard ourselves as licensed torturers of the rest of creation; that we cannot, for our own sakes, afford it.' If those who question the ability of evil to produce good are right, it might well be suggested that mankind's psychological sickness, now greater than ever before, is evidence enough that we do not get away with flying in the face of natural rules.

Bernard Shaw put the humanistic argument reasonably enough when he asked that if animals are tortured for the small amount of knowledge that may be gained from their suffering, what greater knowledge may not be acquired from vivisectional research on man himself. The question turned out to be prophetic, for medical journals have since supplied irrefutable evidence of a growing acceptance of the use of 'human guinea pigs', many of them being moribund, delirious, psychotic or comatose patients, or infants and children, and none in a position to give legally valid consent.

However, no one who supports the practice of animal vivisection has any logical justification for objecting to human subjects being used, and in fairness to the orthodox medical profession it must be pointed out that no surgeon can be launched on his career without at some point having to make his first incision in the body of a living patient. This in itself is a form of experiment which, however supervised, carries a distinct element of risk to the 'guinea pig', as anyone who has worked in the operating theatres of the teaching hospitals is particularly well qualified to confirm.

It is, therefore, the basis that needs to be argued, rather than the case for human versus animal experimentation or degrees of either. Aldous Huxley put the matter concisely when he said that the means employed determine the nature of the ends produced. The materialist may write off such a statement as irrelevant philosophising, but the law of cause and effect cannot be dispelled by scientific sophistry. Indeed, it is surprising—or it would be if humanity's capacity for self-deception was not so painfully apparent—that medical orthodoxy has not recognised the distinctly possible link between the inhuman methods of much medical research and the grindingly slow advance in so many areas of knowledge that have depended upon the fundamentally *un*scientific methods of vivisection. Yet the slightest suggestion that the vivisectional basis of orthodox medicine should be questioned provokes the fiercest antagonism from many of its proponents. Such reactions may well be evidence of the subconscious conflict in the minds of men and women attempting the ultimately impossible task of achieving good ends by reliance upon evolutionarily indefensible methods.

Admittedly one is in the field of conjecture at this point, but it is at least arguable that a naturally conservative body of educated people, many schooled in middle-class ethical traditions, are victims of a conflict between, on the one hand, a conventional and often religious upbringing in which at least lip service was paid to the belief that good cannot result from evil, and on the other the requirements made upon them to practise, or at least rely upon, experimentation involving a greater intensification of calculated suffering than anything else we deliberately inflict on defenceless sentient creatures.

If this suggestion has substance, the bitter antagonism of some defenders of vivisection may well be evidence of chinks in the armour, for it is reasonable to assume that practitioners who are entirely assured of the blamelessness of their methods and of the inefficacy of alternative lines of research, would not evince such extreme detestation of criticism were they not at least subsconsciously aware of a fearsome dichotomy lying at the roots of their profession. But outside their specialism many medical people are intelligent and informed men and women, and it would be absurd of the critics of vivisection to suggest that most practising G.P.s, the nursing services and countless people doing admirable and well-intentioned work for the welfare of others were anything but sincere and, in intent, ethical and even idealistic citizens.

Let this be repeated—it would be wrong and absurd to see such people as callous monsters. Even those closest to the realities of the research laboratories should be seen (with the exception of that minority of sadistic and perverted personalities that infiltrates every human activity) as guilty more of being brain-washed by the orthodoxies of a singularly inflexible and self-satisfied branch of the 'System' than of taking pleasure in inflicting suffering for its own sake.

For the more responsible and concerned members of that body of general practitioners, physicians and surgeons, the very existence of so dichotomous a basis to their specialism makes their efforts all the more difficult in a world wherein knowledge and education, for all its limitations, is making a significant minority of laymen more aware of the inconsistencies, contradictions and motivations in professional and commercial conduct. In fact, it might well be argued that the medical profession will before long be in fierce and conscious need of an alternative to vivisection, and already there is evidence of a growing interest in the use of tissue culture and diploid or other isolated cells as a substitute for animal experimentation. The Lawson Tait Medical and Scientific Research Trust in Harley Street, London, is but one body representing distinguished medical and scientific experts who see, and work for, how the wind is changing.

It is hopeful that the strongest criticisms of vivisection have for long come from among the medical profession itself. Many quotations are possible, but one of the most revealing and frank statements comes from the famous Hungarian medical scientist Dr. Szent-Gyorgi who has said:

> The desire to alleviate suffering is of small value in research—such a person should be advised to work for a charity. Research wants egotists, damn egotists, who seek their own pleasure and satisfaction, but find it in solving the puzzles of nature.

Had that come from an anti-vivisectionist layman, no degree of condemnation would have been too strong for such 'cynicism'! But it is the kind of other-side-of-the-coin observation that is essential if one is to get balance into one's evaluations. For instance, it takes no great degree of education to detect the monstrous and callous absurdity of a society that chooses to over-indulge and pollute its way into physical and mental ill-health, and then tortures millions of animals in order to find answers to diseases that could so often be prevented by a change of habit. Perhaps the 21st-century's symbol of contemporary insanity will be the twitching tail-ends of a dozen imprisoned white mice being compelled to inhale tobacco smoke until they develop the cancers that human beings invite in preference to the rejection of an addiction that no self-respecting mouse would give skirting room to.

It would be easy to wind up this theme by citing evidence of the degree of pitiless insensitivity of which many practising vivisectors are capable. It would be simple to prove that men have something to hide when they choose to report that 'a stress-producing stimulus provoked repeated vocalisation'. But stirring mere animosity is pointless, and the facts are recorded for those who need them. It is more constructive to see such people as victims of society's willingness to exact from the defenceless any price for its own supposed well-being. Society is only too willing to believe the fringe lies, euphemisms and distortions that surround its less excusable practices, among which has for long been the totally false assumption that, in this country at least, Government inspection of laboratories ensures that there is an acceptable limit to what goes on. That that inspectorate is woefully inadequate is better known to vivisectors than to anyone else, and even in Great Britain, where there is at least some legislation to give pause for thought that would not even get off the ground in Japan, America or the Catholic countries of the world, the law for the protection of animals' 'rights' is such that there is virtually no experiment that cannot be performed by those who know the ropes and the paperwork.

But the case against vivisection rests not on such minutiae, depressing though they are, nor on the fact that it often fails to find a cure, or even a palliative, for some ill. If it has only once succeeded there will be someone prepared to argue that it is therefore justified. Again to quote Shaw, the argument is not between success and failure any more than it is between the legitimacy of vivisecting quadrupeds or bipeds. It is over human conduct. This returns us inexorably to the only argument against vivisection that will be seen to have lasting power—that we do not improve human society by means that debase human character.

When mankind can bring itself to accept that simple but overwhelmingly important fact (or natural law, as it has already been described), then and only then will progress cease to be confused with opportunism, and the basis of civilisation will have been laid.

But to return to the point that prompted that necessary digression into the ethics of vivisection, no suggestion is being made that we should *not* be concerned about battered babies and every other example of the violence and brutality in society. The nonsense and wickedness lies in suggesting that it has to be an either/or concern. There is, in fact, already considerable dismay over many forms of cruelty to our own species (even if much of it is confined within national boundaries and is on a domestic level), and no proposal is now being made that one should drop one's concern for battered babies in favour of battered animals. Rather, the assertion is that we should be concerned with the whole wide spectrum of man's bestiality and not be content to tackle it piecemeal in only those spheres where man himself sees an immediate benefit to his own species, or in a field where no self-sacrifice is necessary.

This is, surely, the one vital ingredient missing in so much of the rightly expressed anxiety about over-population, pollution, violence, exploitation and their concomitant ills—a *total* concern. With few exceptions, those demographers, conservationists, ecologists, scientists, economists, et cetera, who are aware of the perils reveal a concern that is entirely over the future of our own species. If a concern is expressed for other species, this is invariably because maintaining the balance among, or the location of, those species is desirable in *man's* interest.

Unless we can learn to think and feel in totality, not sectionally and compartmentally, we shall never arrive at total or even workable solutions. For compartmental thinking, sectional concern, qualified objectives—these, or the half-baked thinking behind them, are precisely what have brought us to the present situation. It has been the greed of the industrialist, the blinkered wisdom of the economist, the power-seeking ambition of politicians, the specious self-interest of advertisers, the cynical triviality of many journalists and exponents of the arts, the narrow intolerance of religionists, and the in-turned selfishness and apathy of Mr. Average Man, that have created the human condition of which we now have good reason to complain.

This is one of those naked facts that are so obvious that future generations, if we beget them, will look back and say: 'Why on earth didn't they realise that and do something about it before reaching such a desperate situation?' Unfortunately life teaches us that the majority is far more interested in the irrelevancies than in the obvious. The irrelevancies provide distraction. The obvious demands effort. The obvious of today is such, however, that we cannot much longer accept the specious dictum of 'Have your cake and eat it', for this holds water only for so long as it is possible to lay hands on the cake's ingredients.

We are nearly all on the make for 'Number One'. Call it common sense, call it survival-technique, call it Christianity or what-you-will, but the time is overdue when we must start to think also about numbers Two, Three and Four. The process has begun—one can be grateful for that

—but it is still far from showing that totality of concern that would prove man's long-alleged superiority over the animals by inspiring in him an interest over their welfare that is based not merely on 'what's in it for man', but also on the realisation of a pattern for progress that obliges him to treat his total surroundings with a meaningful compassion. In days gone by such a compassion would have been seen within a religious context, if it had been seen at all. Today we are sufficiently well-informed to see both the good sense and the obligation implicit in the discipline of—to suggest a re-phrasing, for our age, of the 'Golden Rule'—'Doing unto our surroundings as we would do unto ourselves.'

FIVE

God's in Our Heaven

To regard man, the most ephemeral and rapidly evolving of all species, as the final and unsurpassable achievement of creation, especially at his present-day particularly dangerous and disagreeable state of development, is certainly the most arrogant and dangerous of all untenable doctrines. If I thought of man as the final image of God, I should not know what to think of God. But when I consider that our ancestors, at a time fairly recent in relation to the earth's history, were perfectly ordinary apes, closely related to chimpanzees, I see a glimmer of hope. It does not require very great optimism to assume that from us human beings something better and higher may evolve. Far from seeing in man the irrevocable and unsurpassable image of God, I assert —more modestly and, I believe, in greater awe of the Creation and its infinite possibilities—that the long-sought missing link between animals and the really humane being is ourselves!

KONRAD LORENZ: *On Aggression*

THE YOUNG, IT IS BEING SAID, need a new religion. One might add: 'And not only the young.' For religion, unconfined by sectarian apathy, prejudice and intolerance, means a state of life consciously governed by accepted principles. If we are agreed that what most of us lack today is a sense of direction, and identification and co-ordination of effort with a logical and satisfying aim in mind, then what we lack and need is indeed religion. Having said which, let it be stressed again that this is not the thin end of a wedge for the championing of any fixed sectarian belief. Organisationalism's worst excesses and injustices have been mile-stoned by sectarian labels.

Words are notorious for restricting our thinking and provoking our antagonisms. So already one seeks to get away from the very word 'religion' with all its connotations. But so dominated are most of us by our language and upbringing that as soon as one word is rejected another, equally associative and restricting, is likely to spring up in its place. Eventually we have to settle on one or other of these irritants, examine it, and try to manipulate it to create a lead-in to what one is trying to say.

Probably the least restrictive, because the most over-interpreted, of these provoking nouns is the word 'God'. A hundred and one associative concepts immediately come to mind, but God is perhaps the best term to start off with, if for no better reason than that we all, in some form or other, acknowledge God or a god. Zeus, Mazda, Attis, Helios, Apollo, Purusha, Atman, Reality, Creator, Profits, GNP, Sex, Sport, Power, Violence, Liquor, Drugs, these are all synonyms for god (with or without the capital 'G') in the many-sided minds of men.

But if we slide over that rather trite observation, it remains true to say that any deeper examination of the function of religious belief reveals that almost without exception 'God' has been associated with the role of Protector. In some religious systems this concept is associated with a vengeful and violent disciplinarian, but the greatest philosophies have leaned almost without exception towards the concept of a deity of compassion and tolerance. Despite its poor performance ever since, even Christianity pays lip service to its original acceptance that God was a god of love.

'But if God is love . . .?' How many of us, young and old, and sensitive to the state of the world and man's place therein, have prefaced our doubt by such a phrase as this?

Where some words are all too associative and restricting, others—such as 'liberty', 'spiritual', 'freedom', 'love' and 'rights'—are so open to individual interpretation that either they must be defined or they must be rejected for some word or set of words than can be used more successfully. 'Spiritual', for instance, is probably more often used to describe some essentially earth-bound exercise of the mind or senses than those more metaphysical (not necessarily mystical) states of consciousness that can properly lay claim to the term. If 'God' is another word more open to abuse and interpretation than most, probably the reason for this is that ever since the dawn of man he has found the need to respect some power higher than himself. Whether he invented it or tuned into it, worshipped it or rejected it, he has kept it alive in all ages and all countries with the result that 'God' is by now meaningless to many and a source of comfort or contention to the rest.

The failure of the Churches to keep up with the times and command the respect they were accorded even only fifty years ago can perhaps be seen to be due as much to their clinging to outworn terminology as to outdated concepts and rituals. Incredibly, even today there must be many millions whose concept of God is anthropomorphic—that of a deity in somewhat human form, perhaps even bearded and sitting on a cloud. And it must be laid against more than one vestry door that the Church has done all too little to dispel this concept. Some of its dignitaries seem to believe in it themselves.

The origins of the anthropomorphic concept are easy enough to trace but need not concern us here. It is taken for granted that the reader finds such a notion unsatisfactory and unthinkable. But if we agree that God is neither an old man in the sky nor some vague all-pervading presence that is at one and the same time all-seeing, all-knowing and capable of intervention in the affairs of men, then what are we left with? Have we not destroyed both the simple and the mystical concepts of God, leaving only a vacuum?

Here, surely, we come up against the crux of our definition, for the one common factor that until the very recent past can be found in all the major religions of the world is that God, whatever his form or present function, was the Something that was responsible for the creation of the world we know and the universe we think we know.

THE RED HERRING OF CREATION

How many of us have said, often at that crucial stage when it is essential to see logic in fundamentals if we are to progress with any conviction or sustained interest to the next stage in belief or purpose: 'But if God is love and created the world, why did he allow its evils, cruelties and injustice?' And how many of us, at precisely that point, received no satisfactory answers from our parents, our teachers or the Church?

Fifty years ago, 'It is a divine mystery,' 'The ways of God are strange,' 'It is not given to us to question,' or 'You'll understand when you are older' were evasions that might have been acceptable to young people brain-washed into the belief that age and authority are invariably synonymous with wisdom. But today explanations have to make sense, and if there is no satisfactory explanation available, then an admission of ignorance will invite more respect than bluster and avoidance tactics. Considering the amount of sophistry that has been employed by the old to control the young, it is a wonder that the baby has not been thrown away with the bath water more often.

What has less frequently been examined is the premise on which the 'But if God is love . . .' sort of question has been based. For after all, what authority have we, except for some Biblical (mostly Old Testament) texts, for assuming that it is necessary to equate or associate the idea of a God with the creation of the physical universe?

Is there any reason why we should not accept, and find sufficient, a concept of God that totally ignores how, when or by what means the material world came into being?

After all, if we look back into history we can only reasonably conclude that 'God' was invented by man to explain the existence of himself and the world he inhabits. 'God' did not say he created the world, man said it. It might also be stressed at this point that neither did Jesus claim to be God. The Church claimed it.

Why, then, insist that creation can only be explained in terms of a conscious Creator? Or if some find it unsatisfactory to visualise creation as the product of anything but some form of conscious mind, need they therefore assume that that creating mind is the same principle, spirit or call-it-what-you-like that, within another context, we term God?

To think on these lines is, clearly, to challenge long-held concepts. Such concepts, like many of our traditions and habits, have been kept alive for so long that many of us never *think* about them at all. We all tend to believe, if questioned, that our habits are the result of our thinking. All too often the contrary is true—our thinking is the result of our habits. 'People,' it has been said with some truth, 'don't think. They only think they think.'

So for the sake of the discussion let us ignore the red herring that has lain, whale-size, in our path for so long. For if we are going to be honest with ourselves we know that we cannot, on the basis of examining the credentials of a God that is equatable with love and concern, imagine for a moment that a loving and concerned Creator could have thought up such a shambles of greed, violence and unhappiness as is revealed by any honest lid-off examination of the total world picture.

But this is not to say that godliness cannot and does not exist, despite the domination of nature red in tooth and claw which we can see all around us if we do not choose to go about in blinkers.

At once we are faced with another definition, that of 'godliness'. But if we can agree that the definition of God as 'a superhuman person who is worshipped as having power over nature and the fortunes of mankind . . . the Creator and Ruler of the Universe' (SOED) be shorn of its anthropomorphic imagery, it becomes easier to accept that godliness is nothing more nor less than the reflection of those qualities that one might reasonably suppose should be found in the active principle of goodness. That God is Good (that is, Good Principle) is an obvious and oft-repeated dictum that has meaning and sense for just as long as we leave it alone. What undermines and destroys the logic of this simple concept is the tampering and sophisticated theology that for 2,000 years has worked up the unequivocal recorded statements of a simple but, so far as we know, essentially honest and good man into the most involved and powerful commercial interest in the world.

If we can agree this far we have reached the point where the oldest question in the world— 'Do you believe in God?' —means quite simply: 'Do you believe that there is a case for living a life, irrespective of our origins and destination (for we *know* nothing of either), that is based on Good Principle?' If the answer to that is, 'Yes, I do', then one is saying no more and no less than that one subscribes to the moral code that is found at the root of nearly every great religion and philosophy that has been born in the mind of man.

In other terms, we could say that we will accept 'God' as synonymous with self-discipline, with duty, with a practical as well as an emotional concern for others and for our responsibilities to them, to ourselves and to our total environment. But not as synonymous with a creator or conscious controller of that small corner of a universe that is totally beyond our pathetically limited understanding.

Perhaps it goes without saying that the reason why organised religion is in so neglected a condition is not that the essence of all great philosophical and religious systems has been found wanting, but that the vast human and often very godless process of creating and running the organisation has taken precedence and has encouraged its members and its followers to forget the simple rules that govern a truly godly (or good) life.

This chapter has attempted little more than the definition of some key words that have been blurred and tarnished by time, and the suggestion that a different approach to the ancient mystery of creation might open up an acceptable viewpoint from which man's arguments over his origins can be seen as largely irrelevant to the question of his purpose and destination. Perhaps the conclusions that have been suggested can be summarised as follows:

1. We do not know, and we do not need to know, the origins of the material world.
2. We do not know, and we do not need to know at this stage in our evolution, our personal or racial destiny.
3. We do know that most of the truly great minds of the past have concluded that it is better to lead a life based on good principle rather than on bad, if for no better reason than that suggested by the somewhat self-interestedly framed 'Golden Rule'— Do unto others as you would have them do unto you.
4. We do know, for observation makes it plain, that man needs some form of faith and purpose to carry him through the often disillusioning and disheartening experiences of life.
5. We know that material evolution is a progressive thing, and it is clear even from man's limited experience that it suggests some kind of purpose, even though the nature of that purpose is not known to us.
6. It is therefore reasonable to suppose that mind is equally capable of evolution and may have a purpose and a destination which as yet we have hardly begun to understand and which may well be beyond the kind of awareness of which we are capable at this stage in our development.
7. In accepting these six points we come as near as it is possible to come, without embarking upon conjecture, to an understanding of man's spiritual purpose (in this context 'spiritual' can be defined as a growing awareness of what life is all about—though mystics have put it more subtly). It is an understanding that is based upon acceptance of the validity of the neglected centre of true philosophy—that we should live our lives according to good principles, leaving the problems of

creation and destiny until such time as it may be necessary, and we may be equipped, to understand them. Whether this time comes in our own day or a thousand years hence is neither here nor there both literally and philosophically. The important thing is to be on the right road; to see the need to attain a personal excellence by acceptance of, and fidelity to, a moral code. In short, to have what we all need—the security of a discipline, a framework and a sense of purpose, whether or not we may individually conceive of an ultimate destination.

SIX

The Sickly Substitute

Man without law is the lowest of the animals.

ARISTOTLE

Young people now love luxury, they have bad manners, contempt for authority; they have become tyrants in the household. They contradict their parents and tyrannise their teachers.

SOCRATES in 400 B.C.

It's all that the young can do for the old, to shock them and keep them up to date.

G. B. SHAW: *Fanny's First Play*

The good of the people is the chief law.

CICERO

THE GOOD OF THE PEOPLE (in Cicero's sense, what is good *for* the people) is inextricably bound up with that personal excellence (that good *in* the people) referred to on the previous page, and it is in man's basic need to acquire a sense of individual purpose and to be conscious of his ability and obligation to play a meaningful part in the evolutionary process, that his main hope lies. This, finally, must be the answer to his over-valued technology and to the cultural sickness that marks the decline of civilisations. This sickness is depressingly apparent at the present time, but unless society chooses to abrogate reason completely and permanently, which must seem improbable even to the most hardened pessimist, it is scarcely on the cards that the monotonous anti-life philosophy of our so-called Permissive Society's spokesmen can do more than produce a temporary evolutionary set-back.

The rapidity and eagerness with which some sections of society have welcomed the licence they mistake for freedom will doubtless not astonish impartial later historians who, in tracing the course of 20th-century Western civilisation, are unlikely to overlook the unsurprising fact that two world wars and their spiritual casualties made a major contribution to what is perhaps the first widely organised and purposive attempt to corrupt the character of entire nations by planting in a willing or unsuspecting host a virus more subtle and more fundamentally destructive than the relative crudities of conventional physical warfare.

Society has always been corrupt, as we well know. The evil that men do lives after them now as it has always done. But although evil men have planned evil acts throughout history, and although the wars of this century were quite obviously not symptoms of a humane and successfully conducted civilisation, it is only quite recently that we have witnessed the pathetic and despicable attempts of cultural and commercial interests to foster quite knowingly and deliberately a sickness in the soul of man.

The fostering has been helped along by the pseudo-psychologists of the you-can't-help-being-what-you-are school, whose over-simplification of the concept of freedom in the zanier areas of atheistic existentialism have sounded plausible enough to deceive or confuse many who argue at the surface level of philosophy. But although the French have coined phrases covering most aspects of *la condition humaine,* the meaning behind *tout comprendre c'est tout pardonner* should not be so perverted that we accept the naïve supposition that mankind is so much the product of his genes, his upbringing and even his physiognomy that he lacks free choice and is the unwitting slave of his impulses and subconscious promptings. Such wishful unreasoning, based on a peck of knowledge but unbalanced by overstatement, must be seen for what it is, for in the artless and very young it has an obvious appeal, too easily cancelling healthy, needed criticism and removing incentive for that self-improvement that is the prerequisite of social reform.

Having raised that emotive slogan 'The Permissive Society', a distinction must be made. The natural rebellion of youth—the Dismissive Society—is one thing, and heaven help the society in which young people no longer question the actions and acceptances of their elders. Their rebellion is a phenomenon we have always known about but never, at least as parents, seem to be able to take for granted. If even Socrates, who had plenty of time for contemplation, could run on about the behaviour of youth, it is hardly surprising that mere parents of today should be so slow to realise just how much good it may be doing them to have their ideas shaken up by the negativity of adolescent argument and contempt.

But the anything-goes and patently unbalanced anti-philosophy of the proponents of total permissiveness is something a good deal different. Even Socrates did not have to tackle such commercially motivated cultivation of violence, self-abuse, loveless promiscuity, ugliness and half-baked thinking as that which threatens to dominate the sick culture of our day. Only recently has it been suggested that permissiveness should be the end product of dismissiveness.

In Socrates' time, if you wanted a reputation for being a thinker, you had to work for it. What you thought might or might not be accepted by your contemporaries, but it tended (if it achieved sufficient permanence to survive to this day) to be consistent and coherent, moving from a given premise to a logical conclusion.

Much of today's thinking, if it can be dignified by such a term, is of a very different quality. Today we pay our respects to the 'expert', the 'specialist' or the 'consultant' in this or that—sometimes, undeniably, for services satisfactorily rendered, but all too often without allowance for the remarkably obvious though too easily forgotten fact that a specialist in anything is by definition limited in his interests and therefore his judgments. Our culture is distorted by the shallow and half-formed thinking of over-night personalities ambitious for easy reputations and the material rewards that are the result. Whizz-kids of the New Mood, urbanised, under-exercised, and intellectually blinkered from excessive attention to the West's most genitallyobsessed writers, psycho-analysts and (which is worse) their interpreters.

'They'll grow up,' say the optimists, and Alphonse Karr's *Plus ça change, plus c'est la même chose* was fair comment not only on the repetitious pageant of human life, but also on those perennially new judgments of writers and sociologists who, like the rest of us, have had to discover the hard way (that is, by living) that mankind's social progress depends upon outgrowing that phase of negative anarchy that often sprouts with, or even before, the pubic hair. However, not all of us mature just because we grow older. The graph of arrested development has not noticeably plunged since the onset of mass education. Although there have always been grand old men of violence, exploitation, and artistic or literary innovation whom society will excuse anything so long as the personality is 'big' enough, there is now an inbred fraternity of grand old men of diminished judgments and enlarged prostates whose obsessive but shallow intellectual attainments, undeserving of literary or artistic assessment, are adequate to command respectful, if dim-witted, audiences.

For although a lot has been said in this book that sets high store on the importance of intellect, the anti-intellectual case must be firmly stated. There are no more dangerous men and women in the world than specialist intellectuals, whether they move in the higher cultural strata of society or are the dogsbodies of a popular press with briefs to distort, select and colour news by the introduction of friction, personalities and sensationalism. Specialism means that there is an axe to grind, a personal kink to justify, or simply a product to sell. Specialism in selling baked beans does limited harm. Specialism in selling guidelines for human behaviour can do enormous damage unless those guidelines radiate so widely and from so selfless a concern that their very variety, range and coherence transcend the limitations of specialism.

Many specialists do little harm because their intellectual level is so naïve and their unbalance so obvious and lacking in appeal. Nowadays the kill-to-cure exhortations of the professional military and the chameleon promises of party politicians fool only the most indolent and innocent. The specialists who can do real damage are those whose intellectualism relies on specious half-truth and lacks that breadth of concern and moral integrity that can only come from a balanced personality in which emotional judgments have been permitted their due place in harmony with a mature mind.

Evidence of the importance of such balance may be seen in D. H. Lawrence, whose literary output ranged from the painfully banal to the indisputably brilliant, and who was a life-long slave to his sexuality and profoundly incapable of making mature and lasting relationships with others, sexually or intellectually. In view of the often uncritical and uninformed enthusiasm his writings have attracted, it is a pity that it has not been faced and emphasised more often that Lawrence fell short in ability or intention to be a major prophet or even a very objective or wide-ranging commentator on the values of his generation. It is easy to be dazzled by sincerely felt or seemingly profound phrases, especially when these are presented to us at an impressionable age as being the quintessence of aesthetic or sensory perceptiveness; but while Lawrence wrote much that is worthy of study and respect, he was as capable as are most fluent writers of speaking for effect and of relishing a well-turned phrase for its shape and emotional impact as much as for its profundity. There are writers who carry us along with their words rather than with their meaning. They are more usually poets than philosophers.

It was, unfortunately, the imprecision, hysteria and half-thinking behind much of Lawrence's writing that gave his disciples and interpreters the opportunity to build a shallow philosophy (shored up by such established bulwarks as Freud and his innumerable satellites) that, based on a misconception of the nature and purpose of freedom, has produced a culture in which liberty stands for licence, lack of self-discipline, selfishness, lust above love, and the transient joys of appetite over that balanced state of awareness in which all physical and mental pursuits have their place and purpose and ensure a greater freedom (because a better *balance*) than is ever experienced by the abuse of drugs and a sick obsession with violence and the basically tiny repertoire of genital potentialities.

This is not to suggest that Lawrence would necessarily

have approved of this state of things any more (and the comparison goes no further than the end of this sentence) than Jesus Christ would have approved of the Established Church.

His responsibility is more that he allowed words to run away with his thoughts, and that his thoughts were too deeply charged by his own specialism of sexuality. When he charged Puritanism and Calvinism with the dangerous negative religious passion of repression, and with a deep lust for vindictive power over the life-issue ('The Spirit of Place', *English Review*, November 1918), he was putting into the hands of his interpreters meaty material for the equation of 'anti-life' with that ethical and reasoned condition of living from which the Permissive Society is supposed to have rescued us.

Were he alive today Lawrence would in all probability be deeply depressed by the spiritual condition of the so-called civilised world, and he would doubtless accept that his subjective over-concern with the sex motive has been worked up out of all recognition by the least responsible and mature of his successors. Like many men of his temperament (so acutely sharpened by a tubercular constitution), Lawrence suffered deeply from his own sexuality—as, indeed, did his friends and relatives, for he was not the cosiest of companions. These facts are too readily overlooked by those who wish to justify their own 'specialisms' by hiding behind the reputation of a man whose popularity has had so much to do with his being, unwittingly, in the forefront of the 20th-century crusade against the Puritanism of the nineteenth.

It is all too easy, when a respected writer talks good sense (as Lawrence did when, in the context of America's development, he pointed to the severance of the living bond between men and its replacement by that mechanical tie of purposive utility which would inevitably destroy the spontaniety of social union), to feel an obligation to see good sense in what he may have to say on other matters. We all like our gods to be consistent and unanswerable. It is discomforting to be on 'Yes, but . . .' terms with Ultimate Wisdom. It is far easier to feel that we can accept the whole package, especially if stamped and gift-wrapped by contemporary authorities. But life is never as tidy as that unless we are prepared to overlook the gaps left by the difficult bits of the jig-saw.

So selectivity (which is not the same thing as specialism) must never be overlooked. It is the reverse side of the coin of eclecticism. We must weed out before we can opt in. We can applaud Lawrence for his awareness of the 'slow and terrible process of transubstantiation' that has led to the technology-dominated, materialistic and violent society we live in today; but that does not mean that we need also subscribe, say, to his analysis of those inner impulses that led to the migration of those who have been responsible for the 'mechanical monstrosity of the west.' Because Lawrence, as some have put it, 'saw sex in everything', popularising the genitals as organs of thought, this does not preclude later generations from acquiring a better perspective. If they seek one.

In his concern over freedom, Lawrence was not alone in failing to give sufficient weight to the fact that bondage and suppression have seldom aroused as much dislike as mankind's distrust of freedom of choice. Freedom is still a minority persuasion, and although the whole argument of this book depends upon our developing ability to discipline and utilise that most difficult of all conditions of mankind, most of us still react to the burden of liberty and choice as did the little girl in the Montessori kindergarten in Vienna when she asked her teacher: 'Please, Miss, must we again today do what we want to do all day long?'

Any teacher of experience and ability knows that children find security within a framework of discipline, appreciating firmness applied with patience and a sense of humour. Even in their own games children insist upon rigid disciplines and codes of behaviour. They do not want, because they do not feel at ease with, the permissiveness some dishonestly confuse with the considered, positive granting of freedom. Unusually intelligent children may survive a permissive atmosphere, though at some inevitable cost, but the less able are likely to become the delinquents whose origins puzzle (amazingly) those sociologists who can still be heard suggesting nothing better than that we should offer them freedom and tolerance—and wait for them to grow up!

Although there are signs that the pendulum is swinging

back (not, it is to be hoped, the whole way), it is still fashionable to look with horror at the supposed repressiveness of the Victorian era. But while it is true that life then was often, in its way, as brutish, cruel and impersonal as it is today—some would say more so, though this is questionable if one takes into account the push-button wickedness of modern man—there are still many people alive who can testify that, with obvious exceptions, those who were brought up under disciplines now unknown were not less happy than the young of today. Obviously such a statement makes no allowance for the wide-spread misery caused by poverty and exploitation, but it was these evils, and not the rigours of educational methods, that deserve our anger and pity. Among the responsibly educated were many who were in the fortunate position to direct their energies ('sublimate their sexual drive', if the reader prefers) into works of art, science or social service instead of into pointless aggression, vacuous distractions and the less commendable forms of rebellion.

A fearsome lot of nonsense has been talked about the agony of youth facing the incomprehension of its elders, as though adolescence is or ever was for most of us a cheerful, relaxed and confident period of life. That we may, in certain respects, have got through it better 50 or 100 years ago than we do today is proof of little but our present sick self-obsession. It is certainly not proof that the young of today need or deserve the doubtful remedies and palliatives for their 'condition' that the pedlars of subculture are so concerned to pump into them. What, if anything, youth needs is to be left alone by those commercial, political and cultural pressures that have a vested interest in their transition from childhood into what we too often deceive ourselves is maturity. They are the victims not of concern but of exploitation.

The irony of the situation is that the permissiveness by which many of the young imagine they are escaping the establishmentarian values of a capitalist society is nothing less than the calculated product of that society, manufactured and sustained entirely to make profits, whether financial or by way of acquired power and reputation, from the natural rebellion, uncertainty and genital-awareness of the young. Some of them see it, some of them don't, but they are all its victims.

When we talk about the Permissive Society (and how we talk!), what most of us have been conditioned to think about is sex. Or as that is quite a big word if one treats it with a little philological respect, one might more accurately settle for 'genital stimulation' or, as the Victorians would have had it (and they could sometimes be concise), 'lust'. However, 'sex' will serve the present purpose because we can widen its base by seeing that ninety per cent of our sex-centred permissiveness is concerned either with the actual sexual act and its often uncomfortable variations, or with those associative adjuncts and stimulae such as alcohol; tobacco; rich and excessive food; many films, books and magazines; much visual art; fast cars; fashion; and a whole range of chemical products more usually lumped under the heading of drugs than are whisky or (if you enjoy life at the other end of the social spectrum) meths.

In passing, one might wonder how the rocketing population of the industrial revolution ever came about when one sees what little help was then given in coming to terms with what, in gross over-statement, were known as 'the facts of life'—and by some, surprisingly, still are. Yet somehow they contrived to grope their way through the mists of ignorance and repression to lay the basis for that excess of their species which their more environmentally-aware successors now view with justifiable trepidation. Whatever they were doing in those days, and it certainly wasn't watching television, no one hurried to be identified as an active participant in a gloatingly permissive society. 'That Kind of Thing' was symbolised, even only thirty years ago, by furtive men in raincoats shuffling in pavement queues outside the sleazier cinemas. Society accepted that it must suffer its quota of coprophiliacs and had even begun to realise that the maladjusted deserved sympathy and help.

But today, if our journalists, publishers and swinging barristers are to be believed, we are all seeking, indeed avid, to be 'permitted', and carry our maladjustments before us like banners, anxious only for instant recognition of our *nostalgie de la boue*. There is nothing sleazy about us. Ours is the age in which sex is (or should be) the main preoccupation of every age group, right through from pramhood, when Rupert Bear's no longer imagined phallus proves our mature concern to eradicate sex-guilt from the infant mind (probably substituting penis-envy in its place, but don't let us pursue that one), to those blissful twilight years when our senior citizens, pepped into octogenarian full living, are as solid supporters of the rubber playwear manufacturers as any middle-aged one-time blue cinema queuer could have even hoped to be. It is the Big Life. Big and beautiful, so the advertisers say. The beautiful life in the beautiful, bountiful world of maximum consumption wherein anything that can be bought or sold, irrespective of need or even inclination, is the right and obligation of every normal, adjusted man, woman and child.

But are we all such fools as 'they' would have us be? It seems not, for these criticisms reflect a growing body of concern with the absurd distortions of what life is really all about. It is a concern that is to be found not only among those old enough to recall at least a few better aspects of the world of which the young have no memory, but also among the principal victims of these perverted and immature values. Young people are increasingly waking up to, and deeply resenting, the fact that the commercial and cultural purveyors of our gross materialism have less evolutionary justification than bluebottles on offal. The young are recognising the wider obscenity.

So much of that obscenity is sex-centred that it is easy to acquire the habit of equating permissiveness with mere pornography. There is no ignoring the fact that sex is heap-powerful medicine for all of us, and certainly not least for most intellectuals whose heightened powers of thought and imagination, in conjunction with the disadvantages of a sedentary life, can play havoc with their ambitions for that balanced outlook that must be the target for every civilised man and woman.

The flesh is weak and doubtless always will be. But because many of us, in the improbable event of being cornered in a warm bedroom by the lecherous twin of Helen of Troy, might well be tempted to give our evolutionary ambitions the night off, this is no argument for the necessity for hard-core pornography.

What should really disenchant us about hard-core pornography is a clear, level look at hard-core pornographers. The motives and immaturity of such people are usually so obvious as to cement the realisation that if their spur is not profit, then it is a form of spiritual sickness quite as 'clinically' identifiable as other delusional illness. The cultural propagandists for porn invariably argue that sexual permissiveness is the sign of adult status. 'Let us be adult about this' is so often the *cri de cœur* (if coeur be the appropriate organ) of those least qualified to claim that comparatively rare station in life. The immaturity of these sexpots is in direct proportion to their inability to recognise that an adult's responsibility is to hand mature values on to the next generation, not to handicap them by transmitting the virus of unbalance and inadequacy.

The obsessed advocates of limitless sexuality are also recognisable by their inability to learn the difference between eroticism (which has always been with us) and the uglification of sex (without which we can manage quite easily). Eroticism is a form of idealism, even if not on a very high level. As such it does little harm in its right place. Uglification of sex (and perhaps uglification of anything else, come to that) is, on the other hand, a form of perversion and can have no appeal to the balanced individual, whether young or old.

If such observations are seen as statements of the crashingly obvious, then they are right in line with the intention of this book. It has always been the perverse tendency of the over-sophisticated mind to overlook the obvious, and it is an understanding of the obvious that is precisely what our world needs above everything else.

It is that instinctive recognition of the obvious, however imperfectly thought out, that is common among the older critics of the Permissive Society whose revulsion is as a rule based upon religious considerations. We should not too readily scorn this particular road to Rome. If a sound reaction springs from some sectarian-induced awareness of the need for self-discipline and a sense of purpose, it makes no sense to allow an atheistic antagonism to write off the ends because of disagreement with the means. The most balanced society would be a bore and an impossibility without variety.

But for most thoughtful reactors against the unidealistic and monotonous values of the permissive society, the matter boils down to balance rather than morality in the conventional sense. It is that lack of balance that is the most obvious symptom of society's malaise. For a moment we can return to D. H. Lawrence, for it was precisely his own considerable lack of balance by which his more uncritical followers have been blinded. A sense of balance is inseparable from, perhaps even synonymous with, a sense of humour, and this is one element that was almost totally absent from Lawrence's make-up. One should be careful about people who lack this vital ingredient, for an awareness of the ridiculous (in oneself, in others, in the entire tragi-comedy of human life) is an absolute essential to the balanced personality. Too much of it, it is true, can bring sex, in its narrower sense, almost to a standstill. Chesterfield's dictum that the pleasure is momentary, the cost prohibitive and the position ridiculous is not the kind of observation most of us care to recall in moments of heightened sensory or romantic perception, but in point of fact the threat from such dampeners is small, body chemistry being what it is. When the tide of youth's energy is running full, nature has a way of getting over minor intellectual barriers all too successfully if one is to believe the population graphs (and one should).

It would be foolish to underrate the power of that chemistry. The young, not to mention both the commercial and sick-culture salesmen of a capitalist system, are well aware of its strength. Computers have been defined as machines created by Technological Man to ensure that he continues to receive the right answers to the wrong questions, and much the same might be said of our more dedicated devolutionaries—those slaves and promoters of sensory experience whose goal is a world of happy pigs and discontented philosophers; the function of the pigs being indiscriminate guzzling, the rôle of the philosophers being to provide the pigs with doubts from which to escape in ever widening circles of conspicuous consumption and titillation. The courage of one's addictions is a lousy basis for getting through life.

The suggestion is probably filtering through that the real answer to the proponents of the Permissive Society is not that violence, promiscuity, deviation, drug-taking, etc., are immoral or wrong, for such terms are too inexact for many of us now, but simply that because these habits imply a lack of balance, a lack of perspective, a state of weakness, they do not and cannot satisfy and bring happiness. Nothing in nature is 'happy' in a state of unbalance, as we are rapidly learning in our new-found concern over the physical environment. Nor should we have to feel guilty hedonists about wanting happiness. We do and should want happiness both for ourselves and for others. Indeed, happiness is essentially something that needs to be shared if it is to be sustained. Only an insensitive and self-centred oaf can imagine himself to be happy in an atmosphere of others' wretchedness.

But none of us can expect or deserve happiness to be handed to him on a plate. It is a state of mind that has to be earned through self-discipline and a willingness to lose a portion of the ego in the interests of society at large. Nor is this merely to echo the precepts of such supposedly more 'social' religions as Christianity. A more positive concept of happiness is to be found in Buddhism (or the Buddha Dhamma as it is more usually termed by the followers of Buddha's teachings), a way of life that is awakening a growing interest among Westerners unsatisfied by the various systems of dogmas that seem to be the only alternative to an equally displeasing materialism.

For Buddhism is a way to live Reality. For many of us, Buddhism equates with Yoga, and with its lower reaches, or Hatha Yoga, at that. But while the bodily control that is to be found through the āsanas of Yoga may well be an advance on conventional 'gym', none of the further stages towards Nirvāna can be experienced without the acceptance and practice of Ahimsā (= not hurting; compassion, especially towards non-human species) and its more positive counterpart Karunā (or active compassion) which with Prajñā (transcendental wisdom) make the 'two pillars' of Mahāyāna Buddhism.

Because for so many people Buddhism is nothing more than 'contemplating one's navel', it is frequently written off as a passive and self-centred philosophy. This of course is nonsense, as are so many of our superficial ideas of Eastern thought and practice—nonsense aided and abetted by not a few muscular churchmen nurtured on pre-war Rugby football and the O.T.C., for whom all true gooders must be aggressive doers, and be seen as such. This class of critic forgets that the aim of individual self-improvement is the basis of the vast majority of religious beliefs. But it is not the sole answer unless accompanied by a determination to ensure the active percolation of new values into society, and while the so-called Christian world may have a better, or at least more visible, grasp of the art of communication, it does not hold any prerogative, and it is hardly tenable to suggest that each individual Buddhist can have advanced in his faith in total isolation. That Buddhism places greater importance on meditation than do the Christian nations, for most of whom religion consists of little more than singing hymns as a toning-up ritual before tackling the Sunday joint and the news of a singularly worldly world, is not to be denied, and many Westerners are learning the benefits of this discipline. There is no obligation to restrict such meditation to fit the common image of non-active Eastern man. A balance between contemplation and communication (between East and West, as some may see it) is a desirable and surely attainable compromise and is a far more hopeful concept of religious unity than a brace of archbishops seeking common administrative ground over a glass of port.

In a sense, nearly all religion is hedonistic. More exactly, it offers an escape from unhappiness or uncertainty. The alternatives are invariably transitory and unsatisfying. Drugs provide only a temporary escape from unhappiness, making the eventual adjustment all the more difficult, if not impossible; while a religious conviction that complacently sees pain and misery as part of some divine purpose is a singularly obnoxious method of shedding responsibility for reducing the evil in the world. Neither 'answer' is more praiseworthy than the 'you can't change human nature' cliché of the lazy and self-satisfied man who at heart does not really want to. 'Can'ters' are usually 'won'ters' beneath the surface.

As has already been said, when we talk about the Permissive Society we are usually talking about sex and drugs. Less often, about violence. While few of us care to recognise that the verb to permit has several tenses. Tut-tutting over teenage promiscuity is all too often to indulge in enjoyable shock over what is after all only one aspect of a system in which what has previously *not* been permitted (or at least not blessed) is more interesting to the trivial mind than the more significant obscenities that *are* permitted by society as a whole. If we want to knock the Permissive Society, then we might better realise that the problems of an over-populated and polluted world include the moral pollution represented by armies of the mentally ill; the unemployed; old-age pensioners living on the bread-line; slums; wars; revolutions; cruelty to children; the vivisection, consumption and other abuses of tens of millions of sentient creatures; and all the many forms of violence, persecution and exploitation that riddle the entire unregenerate system of mankind. No one who fails to protest actively, and by deed and sacrifice, against the larger obscenity of violence and cruelty and indifference has the right to stand in judgment over the sexual peccadilloes of the bulk of those young people who tend to be lumped under the general heading of The Permissive Society. Equally, neither have the young a sound basis for resenting criticism unless they are prepared to interpret more widely and in a more compassionate sense their slogan 'Make love, not war.'

While movements such as the Festival of Light should not be accused of advocating a return to Victorianism, for the moral hypocrisy of the last century has long been seen as no more praiseworthy than contemporary permissiveness, there is nevertheless a danger that such campaigns reveal aims too narrow to withstand the predictable jibes of their opponents. Once again, eclecticism is the only answer. Specialism, even in one's attack on devolutionary tendencies, can lead to—or at least provoke charges of—lack of balance. It is essential to define one's slogans. If 'No to Permissiveness' means, to 99 out of 100, merely 'No to Sex', then Permissiveness must be given a sub-heading.

The mass media are the worst offenders in creating through slick but trivial labelling an inadequate and unbalanced realisation of the extent of, and remedies for, our dis-ease. Most of us, fortunately for the population explosion, go to the lavatory more often than we copulate. Yet if journalists devoted as much column yardage to the former process as they do to the latter, they would soon be charged with being unnaturally obsessed by a function that is best taken for granted and given minimal publicity.

It is not rational, just because the Bible said it, to dismiss the view that to be carnally minded is death, whereas to be spiritually minded is life and peace, because in point of fact that realisation has been proved time and time again throughout the history of mankind by nations and individuals who have reached the crossroads of choice between the roads of evolution and devolution. Though not everyone who is concerned about the Permissive Society may reason it out this way, most parents and responsible educators have grasped subconsciously at least that this is the crux of the matter, and their unrest therefore centres on the desire to see happiness and balance in the young—a desire that is strengthened daily by the rapidly spiralling evidence of the lack of peace, love and purpose in those who have fallen victim to the purveyors of third-rate values.

Apart from anything else, it is grossly illogical and unscientific to seek to protect our bodies from the pollution of our material environment and in the same breath to suggest that the protection of the mind of the individual from the pollution of his mental environment is an unnecessary concern. Much nonsensical irrelevance can be laid at the door of clinical psychology, but it has helped to provide insights that must compel all responsible educationists to take account of the development of individual personality and the necessity for some control of the mental environment of the child and adolescent. 'Social requirement' is, in many contexts, only an up-dated synonym for 'religious belief'. So be it. This is an age when the names of roses are legion.

It is encouraging that at a time when much of the blame for how things are is being levelled at scientists, the 'philosophical biologists' to be found in that stream of existential philosophy that shows mounting doubts about behaviourist and Freudian psychology are dismissive of mechanistic explanations and are showing a turn against nihilism and moral inversion that puts many of our contemporary dramatists and novelists to shame. Or should!

There are, in short, strong signs of an increasing disbelief in the essentially violent and anti-life virtues of total materialism. More important, there is evidence of the gradual development of a positive belief in an ethic and a way of life that will replace despair with hope, cynicism with faith, emptiness with purpose, and will restore to the individual, at the cost of his long-standing over-reliance upon organisational control, a sense of personal responsibility that cannot help but infuse and transmute the half-baked and spurious values of a sick and fatalistic society.

Consciously among men, as in nature instinctively, there is at last an awareness of the necessity for equilibrium. The threat of ecological disaster, the over-statements of scientific materialism, the sheer frightfulness of so much of our technological achievement and its implications—these and other factors are, it would appear, at last driving into our minds that if the world is to survive it will do so only when men and women sort themselves out. That they must concentrate on this necessity at the lower levels of their physical appetites just as much as in the higher flights of social purpose and spiritual cognition, can be denied only by those who do not want to face demanding facts.

In brief, we are back again to balance. It is the word that hits into one's brain again and again when listening to the pros and cons of our Permissive Society. For there is no balance in those who can see nothing wrong with our world once the local tides of hard-core pornography have been stemmed, any more than there is balance in the minds of those who would argue that the incessant injection of violence, cruelty or loveless sexuality has no lasting effect on man's character. The latter assertion, and it is frequently made, is perhaps one of the most dismally fatuous claims ever to emerge from the addle-pated, for its corollary is that great literature and profound philosophy have no ennobling effect.

It is the same stable of unthink that seeks 'proof' of a tendency to deprave or corrupt, as though evidence rests only in statistics, polls and witness-box admissions. It needs only common sense to tell us that *any* climate of thought must improve or impoverish, deprave or uplift, and encourage or defeat the individuals who comprise a society. If our imagination is up to admitting that a desperately ill victim of hard drugs has been corrupted by his addiction, we should be capable of realising that a generation of young people indoctrinated by a philosophy of loveless and self-indulgent permissiveness will bear the marks of such misdirection without any single pupil being obliged to swear on oath that prostitution, fetishism or necrophilia had no attraction until some particular piece of pornographic rubbish was thrust into the adolescent hand.

We might more accurately judge the claims of those who deny corruptive intent if we weighed them against their motives. 'What's in it for Bloggs?' is a good basis for reviewing the assertions of all salesmen, be they drug manufacturers, politicians, writers, theatrical managers, publishers, artists, brewers, industrialists or the advertising copywriters who represent them. It would be unreasonable not to attribute self-interest to anyone with commercial motives for promoting a product or an idea, and conversely it is surely reasonable to accept—unless one's Freudianism has got quite out of hand—that the concern of responsible parents and educators over the climate in which children now find themselves is as near to selflessness as anything we can find in the world about us. In a book that has not missed the opportunity to understand and, it is hoped, represent the viewpoints of an increasing number of young people, there must be room for presenting at least this aspect of their elders' current thinking. For if being young has its problems (and no one is denying this), so has being a parent and a teacher. Unfortunately this is a fact that few of us can appreciate until we are parents or teachers ourselves.

Parentally speaking, then, it is fairly tough by any standards to see those one has loved through a sizeable slab of one's adult life being subjected to the sick erotic fantasies and other devolutionary influences of the pedlars of fundamentally anti-life values. In a society whose young are exhorted to break from family control at an ever earlier age, it becomes increasingly absurd for the defenders of our sick culture to suggest that the influence of home backgrounds should restore any necessary balance.

Many such defenders will not even go so far as that, seeking instead to suggest that parents' motives for trying to 'protect' their children are rooted in ignorance and envy. However badly many parents undoubtedly attempt to enforce their standards on the young, and however inadequate some of those standards may be, few parents worthy of that responsibility can sanely be supposed to begrudge their children anything likely to bring them true happiness.

It is far nearer the mark to see that what makes responsible parents hopping mad is the realisation that too many people, motivated solely by greed, power or the need for outlets and justification for their own inadequacies, are intent on dragooning the young for mechanistic sex and synthetic euphoria with all the peripheral consumption that goes with it. In short, the old resent seeing the young conned and robbed. Envy doesn't come into it.

All of which is not to suggest that uncritical sympathy should be showered on parents whose only concern is, through their children, to see the present system perpetuated. Anyone who has reached early middle life in sustained belief that there is nothing needing to be changed deserves sympathy for little else but a degree of unperception bordering on the ga-ga. Yet it is unfortunately true that many adults are too lazy, short-sighted and self-centred to seek either social or self-improvement, being entirely content with their appetites, their habits, and those prejudices they have long substituted for thought. It is therefore understandable that the young are often tempted to throw away the 'baby' of their parents' concern with the 'bathwater' of their shut-minded rigidity and insensitivity.

What understandably maddens so many young people is the hypocrisy of parents who condemn in the young what they tolerate and even admire in their own contemporaries. There is something singularly absurd about quasi-pacificist criticisms of student revolt when they come from men or women whose proudest memories are of their participation in the holocaust of 1939-1945 or the continuing obscenity of the carnage in Vietnam. Equally unappealing are the anti-drug strictures of a parent or educationist who is himself a willing victim and defender of the brewers and tobacco companies. The moral cowardice of those who have not made even a partial stand against such anti-social social patterns as the cocktail party or nightly sessions in the boozer may be explained, if not excused, by an understanding of the compulsions on herd-man to be 'like the other chap' and refrain from 'offending', but it is a sign of some progress if there is at least the admission that addling one's mind, dulling one's reflexes and often ruining one's health is proof not of manliness, virility or necessity, but merely of an inability or unwillingness to question the sillier mores of society.

Colour supplements devoted to scourging our Sunday consciences with the Cathies and Ednas of the system would make more convincing reading if every other page was not devoted to selling the absurd proposition that maturity, judgment and sex appeal are beyond reach until we have a cigarette in one hand, a glass in the other, and a foot pressed hard on the accelerator pedal of one's virility symbol.

But if it is the duty of advertisers to sell hardest what we need the least, it lies in the hands of educationists to counter-advertise by seeing that the latest generation is helped to resist that callous commercialism that knows too well how to exploit the weaknesses of the young. For it is the young who must be the chief concern of a responsible society; once over the 'top' of what passes for a mature age, few people are prepared to make any radical change in their patterns of thought and behaviour.

Total over-night success in strengthening the values and judgments of the young is too much to hope for, but at least the effort of more positive action would gain greater respect for educationists than their own participation in behavioural patterns that remove any basis or qualification for that education in values that at present is so dismally overshadowed by instruction in the rules of avarice and personal advancement on a merely material level. The young do not respect elders who themselves lack standards and consistency. There is something especially distasteful in the sight of middle-aged men and women falling over backwards to reject, qualify or apologise for principles or values, equating tolerance with their own apathy and fear of being thought 'different' or out of touch. Keeping *in* touch rests not in lowering one's own standards, but in seeking a common basis for positive action towards those objectives that at heart we share. Among the shared objectives of all ages is a sense of purpose and fulfilment, and in the majority of cases the realisation that we are all in the same boat and need to accept the discipline of certain standards of conduct is diminished only temporarily by the whipped-up distortions of those concerned to exploit young people at a time in life when reconciliation to the problems of the adult world is most hampered by lack of experience, true self-confidence, and that period of sexual anarchy that makes mature judgments the exception rather than the rule.

For the problem of the generation gap has always been with us, and only wide acceptance of the necessity for, and implications of, eclecticism is going to throw a few planks across the void. Those planks must come from both sides. If fear of change is the charge that can be laid at the door of the old, then equally it can be said of many young people that they have sought too often to *provoke* by the assertion of trivialities and irrelevancies, and too seldom to *reform* by proposing workable and responsible alternatives to the system they despise. It would not matter if they wore their hair down to their shoeless toes if from behind that zariba of hirsute expressionism could come evidence of a genuine and reasoned concern with the basic faults of society, and proof of personal determination to contribute to a better world—not by violence, promiscuity, drugs and other negative symbols of weakness and futility, but by individual reappraisment and effort.

Thankfully, such proof is not lacking, and for every member of the young generation who has successfully thought through to a new pattern or goal, it is reasonable to believe that there must be ten or a hundred times as many who would grasp at the opportunity to make a more positive contribution to the creation of an alternative structure if their educators were prepared to help them to see the first rung of the ladder and to visualise how the world could be if mankind will only unite in realisation of what the word 'civilisation' really means.

SEVEN

The New Plague

Not to be born is best.

SOPHOCLES : *Oedipus Coloneus*

If television and the cinema have done nothing else of merit, they have at least helped to dispel the quaint belief that our species deserves congratulations on 'the dignity of man'. But it is not so much the opportunities we have to witness the ludicrous and bestial antics of the human animal that have destroyed the illusion of our dignity, as the many glimpses we are given of the sheer weight of our numbers. The observer who can see dignity in massed mankind, whether taking its pleasures in some stadium, or eking out its misery in a teeming slum or delta, could put his imagination to better use.

Thankfully, among the less-than-deadly sins pomposity has had a good many knocks in the past few years, and it is at last being generally accepted that the greatest single world problem of our times is the spread of our own species. As is often the case, what was the despised and constantly muzzled opinion of so-called cranks yesterday is the respected wisdom of an increasing number of scientists and sociologists today. Even the politicians have begun to admit that control of our numbers is relevant to a continued, or at least endurable, existence.

As an example of where blind materialism has led us,

the population crisis stands supreme. In our vanity and short-term greed, and despite all too visible writing on innumerable walls, we have allowed the infestation of our species to go uncurbed and unquestioned. Church and State, with that calculated myopia that invites the contempt and suspicion of anyone who does his own thinking, have been at pains to ignore the facts and their implications. Promulgating the questionable notion that there is some special sanctity in human life—a conceit that disappears rapidly in times of war—the churches have long held that man has the inalienable right to perpetuate himself without restraint. Lamentably, at least one major religion still subscribes totally to this unequivocal viewpoint, its concern for the quality of life being clearly subservient to its determination to gain control by sheer weight of numbers. For although there has been some criticism of the Pope's condemnation of all artificial methods of birth control, one fundamental justification for the encyclical has been deafeningly ignored. It has always been the avowed intention of the Roman Catholic Church to dominate the spiritual climate of the world. This ambition depends upon multiplication of its followers. It is difficult to imagine anything more joyfully acceptable to the Catholic hierarchy than a world in which responsible Protestants are falling over backwards to control their numbers. Such are the churches' powers of thought-control that this naïveté over the motives of the Vatican has been virtually unquestioned.

Such realisations of the devious nature of man must be brought into the open if the vast problem of over-population is ever to be tackled realistically and with hope of success. The churches and their laws have been created by man. Man parading as God, maybe, but man all the same. Only man will change them. If he fails to do so, he will have failed both himself and any reasonable concept of god-fearing (good-loving is a better term) behaviour.

As yet all too few people are capable of taking more than a sectional view of the population problem. They can see the separate problems of traffic congestion, urbanisation, despoiled countryside, pollution, and so on, without a full appreciation of the fact that these social ills are only the symptoms of the fundamental problem of racial excess. Party politicians are largely to blame for this, the housing shortage and clean rivers being a more vote-catching platform than an appeal to limit the voters' numbers, but even some of the organisations set up to study and promote conservation and population control are being infiltrated by those who are more concerned to make temporary adjustments to the problems of a rising population than to outline and educate for that actual stabilisation and reduction in numbers that is the only realistic and civilised solution. Unfortunately, a rising population creates jobs for the boys, be they architects, artisans or shopkeepers, and only widespread education in the necessity to be responsible towards our children's children's generation as much as towards our own can dispel that commercially-prompted apathy and antagonism that is no less powerful than the vested inertia of the churches, the political arena, and that large section of the world's inhabitants who prefer to copulate without thought for the calendar, contraceptives or tomorrow.

But a more enlightened and honest approach to these matters is coming because it has to come—though whether it will come in time is entirely up to each one of us. We have reached a point where our spiritual and mental health is in such bad shape that governments must help to turn the tide by bringing in disincentives and even legislation and by prompting a reversal of the trend to uncontrolled urbanisation and the sacrifice of quality to the insatiable god of quantity. No one could now seriously suggest that such thinking should be equated with fascism and a Neitzchean concept of superman. We are faced by stark ecological facts that cannot be ignored. The crisis of population is the biggest challenge to our purely material problems of balance in the world today.

For this reason, it would be easy enough to expand this short section into a two-volume study. But that would be beyond the brief that has been set. Many books are being published by those far better qualified to present the facts of mankind's physical predicament. In proposing the civilised alternative, the concern is to stress the connection between population excess and the issues raised in this book. That connection is inextricably interlocked and will be obvious to anyone who has read (and understood) this far.

EIGHT

The Grab Society

What experience and history teach us is this—that people and governments have never learnt anything from history, or acted on principles deduced from it.

G. W. F. HEGEL

The world is too much with us; late and soon,
Getting and spending, we lay waste our powers . . .

WILLIAM WORDSWORTH

LATER OBSERVERS HAVE PUT the same point more brutally than Wordsworth, but the syntax of poets tends to live longer in man's memory. In the present, the phrase 'We live in a materialistic age' is as often as not trotted out with an air of complacency rather than of lament, or in that uninvolved and objective manner of those sociological boffins who appear to believe that there is some innate and final good in the bare discovery and recording of fact—a good that relieves the discoverer of any responsibility to act on his findings and relate them to his behaviour or pattern of thought. Bad philosophers, bad sociologists, bad scientists—they are all content merely to record.

Much of this is becoming apparent, and of concern, to all age groups, but most hopefully among the young. They have begun to have serious doubts about the unqualified joys of total materialism. Much has been said on this subject in the other chapters of this book, but in the interests of that eminently desirable balance whose virtues have been emphasised as much as the drawbacks to materialism, we should bear in mind that materialism has several faces. We are all, willy-nilly, materialists without choice, in that we are tied to bodies needing constant attention. A boy, a bull, a buttercup, as our early childhood reading constantly reminded us, are all material and can hardly be condemned for being so. Where materialism becomes ugly and anti-life is in its pursuit as an end. There is a significant gulf between the placid materialism of the man who accepts each day at its face value and is content to support his needs within the limitations of an unambitious responsibility, and the aggressive, acquisitive materialism of those who seek, as ends in themselves, as large a hunk of goods and power as their wits can command.

It is wholly understandable that this overt materialism, so much a feature of the capitalist societies, should be detested by those who realise how unevenly the world's goods are distributed, and it is not surprising that many seek an answer in ideologies that purport to stand for more equal distribution of the earth's resources and by-products. But although capitalism offers a splendid target and whipping-boy, many who have taken their studies in a little more depth have come to the conclusion that the two major political systems in the world today, although allegedly in opposition, have more in common than either side is willing to admit. Certainly few would claim that Communism is a jot less materialistic than capitalism, any more than that it has been successful in doing away with differences of class and wealth.

It may be added at this point that comparisons of class and wealth (which are usually synonymous in the minds of those who care most about them) are among the major weapons of provocation in both national and party politics. But the more percipient are seeing that class is a term we tend to define far too narrowly. It reaches well beyond income brackets and accent. Indeed, it would be less misleading to talk of difference-structure rather than of class-structure, for it is differences that make divisions, and differences are legion. It is sad to note how each generation of the politically-minded wastes enormous energy and time agonising over the trivialities of class. So many of us still seem to imagine that distinctions can be made to disappear through increased political activity or legislation. This is an utterly false and hopeless notion. Only as we become more eclectic in our outlook and interests—which is to say, only as we become better educated in the broader and proper sense of that word—will we cease to lend undue importance to surface differences of accent, income, interests, et cetera. That these differences have their importance and drawbacks, it would be foolish to deny. But a totally levelled out and egalitarian society is as much of an impossibility as it would be a bore. Individuals and groups, unless our scientists succeed in producing a race of automata, will always divide themselves into 'classes'—nationally, regionally, domestically, occupationally, culturally, and almost certainly fiscally and racially. What is important and is deserving of the concern and action of everyone who is genuinely committed to make a bigger contribution than a roomful of hot air, is that none of us should allow these minor differences (and they *are* minor compared to the fundamental problems we have to tackle) to get in the way of reforms and ideals that can bring benefit and true progress to the human race generally. The pecking order has been with us ever since the cave was our home and its purlieus our boundary. It is society's responsibility to impose restraints on what is allowed within that pecking order, and in time to replace the sense of peck, as it were, with that better vision of the underlying unity in all life. This would be a more rewarding course than the present futile attempts to war and legislate against man's ineradicable and necessary tendency to detect superficial differences between himself and others.

Such assertions will not be welcome to those who are convinced that reform can only come through political action. Through mis-education, over-population and pressure on the resources of the natural world, all too many of our species remain fiercely wedded to the vice of division and conflict. As has already been suggested, mankind's habit of banding together into groups for corporate action, whether well or evilly intentioned, is possibly his most destructive impulse of all bar the proliferation of his species. When that banding together is led by the young beneath banners urging equality for all, a highly emotive situation can develop. But let us look briefly at this by no means unusual phenomenon in the context of the major political ideologies of our time.

COMMUNAPITALISM

When, as has been said, we examine the claims and actions of Russia and the West today it is increasingly difficult to formulate any clear distinction between them. Communism and Capitalism. How do they differ except in language and geography? Does each label even fit the system as it now operates? If we isolate the political, moral and economic essentials in each and stand them side by side, have we two separate systems or an uneasy, blurred, overlapping admixture that might be more readily recognisable if we coined a new label altogether, such as the hybridised sub-heading above?

Perhaps this is playing with words. But then that is exactly what the Communapitalists do, which is why they have spun such a web of verbiage and confusion around themselves that we are no longer able to tell one from the other except by their rough (often very rough) geographical boundaries.

Like the church, politics depend upon organisations. Upon sections of people prepared to label themselves as This or That and to congregate at appointed times in buildings or open places where the world expects the exponents of Thisism or Thatism to be found—and to expound.

This is all very well for just so long as Thisism or Thatism is in its infancy and has known leaders and spokesmen who have not yet divided and sub-divided, gone over and gone under, replaced and made way, dithered and dispersed, and in short so infused the original concept with muddled thinking, pursuit of power, personal ambition and all the vagaries and treacheries of human motivation that the Thisism and Thatism of yesterday have become the conglomerate Otherology of today.

Take, briefly, the Thisism of Capitalism. Its benefits are short-term and material. Its evils are long-term and spiritual. No one who doubts this will have read this far. But in the absence of any alternative system that can be proved to have been more workable, it is perhaps more realistic to examine the essence of why capitalism has evolved into one of the most dangerous politico-economic systems of our time than to dismiss it out of hand as though thereby it will cease to exist and be replaced by some more noble and hopeful concept on Tuesday week. Instant Nirvāna does not emerge from the mere act of rejection, though the politically naïve of every generation would seem to think it should.

When we examine the basic facts of what might be termed the philosophy of Capitalism we see that, above all, it is a system that responds quickly to man's least praiseworthy motives. For Capitalism is greed. It is also violence and hate and selfishness. In economic terms, it is growth, the economist's euphemism for avarice.

This is as easily said as it is true. Yet it might equally truly be said that the pursuit of profit is a reasonable, even an essential part of human life, for profit is really only the difference between subsistence at the level of a monkey and life at the level of a man in need of those material and influential things of life that should, but do not necessarily, help him along his evolutionary path. When we think of material things we tend to focus on sophisticated kitchen and electrical equipment, furs, jewellery, superfluous gadgetry and gimmickry and on the countless vanities and non-necessities created within a capitalistic society gone mad.

Such aspects of our society's materialism hit few more resounding lows than the teenage magazine, solid with advertisements for vaginal deodorants and make-ups to make love in, with every now and then a small, pious editorial reminder of the homeless and of the inadvisability of being over-concerned about money.

But the important materialisms, surely, are those educational, communicatory and cultural tools, outlets and products that encourage understanding between peoples and enable our species to appreciate its responsibility to one another and to the world around us.

But if the pursuit of profit, by that definition, is not to be wholly condemned, the pursuit of *maximum* profit is an altogether different matter. The pursuit of maximum profit is a destructive and violent abuse of personal and group freedom and is at one and the same time the cornerstone and the canker of most present-day capitalistic activity. Most 'maximums' contain the germ of their own decay. Maximum profit = maximum power = maximum corruption = maximum overthrow of those vital yet fragile threads that hold the fabric of any society together. Where a community exists only by its members living by the maximum exploitation of each other, there is neither substance nor hope. Where principle is subservient to profit, chaos takes over.

It is of course at this point that some have looked with hope at the Thatism of Communism which, like early Socialism, at least pays lip service to the need for communal responsibility and for the control of personal greed and ambition. But already, such is the spread of world communication systems, we know too well that the theory of Communism, like most other theories that get taken over by organisations, bears little relation to the system that exists within Communist nations.

For what *is* Communism? The bulk of British and American 'Communists' neither know what Communism really means nor would enjoy experiencing it at first hand. The material benefits of Communism may well have appeal for impoverished and exploited peasant populations where the difference between life and death may be an ounce of protein, but for the vast majority of Westerners it would represent a downward slope in the graph of material prosperity that would find little favour even among the most militant of shop stewards faced with the obligation to live with wives already converted to washing machines, television, a car, two or more weeks on the Costa Brava, and the other peppermint-flavoured dummies with which an industrial society keeps its workers more or less in the belief that they are contented and fulfilled.

Despite—or perhaps because of—those dummies, for many in the West Communism has become a banner beneath which to show dissatisfaction with the existing state of things in their own country. They have grounds for this dissatisfaction, perhaps stronger grounds than most of them realise. But their 'Communism' is the proof and expression of their disillusion, not of their conversion.

Idealistically, Communism can be compared with the tenets of Christianity. The concept that all property should be vested in the community and labour organised for the common benefit is commendable to say the least, just as was the command of Christ Jesus that we should love one another, or the Buddhist precept of ahimsā.

What is it that happens to the unquestionably right and desirable doctrines that have been laid down again and again by the wisest of men throughout history? Why has the world not grown to be a better and wiser place when the recipe for harmony and happiness between men has so often and so clearly been stated? The answer, if we cared to analyse the short and brutal history of mankind, could occupy many volumes. In this brief study it is only possible to attempt to pinpoint the basic reasons for the world's apparent indifference to the rules of a sane and balanced life. But some useful dialogue, and perhaps even action, may get off the ground if the fundamental basis of these arguments can be objectively and quietly considered by those with a sincere concern.

For when we look squarely at the world around us and begin to see where competitive materialism has got us, it is difficult to claim that the philosophy of materialism, if it can be said to have one, needs no critical examination. Less and less people today would sincerely assert that the world is in no need of some more idealistic and civilised guiding principle. As we know that the guidance is not going to come from the politicians, industry, the military hierarchy or from the bulk of churchmen, most of whom are more interested in the domination of mind than in its dominion, we are left with only one course open to us. It has been stated in this book several times and cannot be over-repeated. Dull though it may sound in a world of instant crisis, over-night decisions and off-the-cuff 'solutions', the answer lies within each one of us.

This is not a palatable truth to those impatiently seeking immediate remedies for long-neglected ills. It is easy to *feel* that more is being done by protest marches and other corporate activities, but though carrying banners, squatting in front of buses, marching and petitioning may be good beginnings, it is fatally easy to accept them as ends. They are, or should be, no more to the protestor than paper, ink and binding is to the author—a vehicle for communication.

Another snag is that there is something that has been bred into many of us—especially if we are British or American—that recoils from so overt a statement as that our goal should be personal excellence. We feel that the suggestion smacks of conceit; that someone is trying to put himself above others; 'Who does he think he is?' springs involuntarily to the lips. There are doubtless several explanations for this, according to our backgrounds, our friendships and our ambitions. The British educational (especially public school) system has a lot to answer for; and in the unspoken requirement, within a Welfare State whose aim always appears to be to level everyone down rather than up, not to rock the boat by talking about achieving higher standards, we are up against one of the wetter blankets that the supporters of a spurious egalitarianism are quick to throw over any suggestion that mankind might be capable of becoming something more than a psychopathic but basically obedient ant.

But all these matters—The Materialistic Society, Communapitalism, Violence, Balance, the Thisisms, the Thatisms and the Whether-or-Nots—can be tackled constructively and rewardingly by the individual prepared to abandon peripheral thinking and observation and give over mind and heart to the task of striking to the roots of the human predicament. Nothing is ever as difficult as the opposers of real progress try to make out. One's only major problem is oneself. The seven deadly sins, and a few more besides, have not ceased to exist just because we may now call them handicaps or social phenomena, and now as of old it is still up to the individual to deal with them as best he can. Although with the rise in education the graffiti of our budding Che Guevaras are to be found ever lower on the lavatory walls, the lineaments of true education have begun to appear. The time to strengthen them is now.

NINE

Please, Teacher

Bankers, priests, lawyers and politicians constitute one class and work together. They do not produce any values, but manipulate values produced by others, and often pass signs for no values at all. Scientists and teachers also comprise a ruling class. They produce the main values mankind has, but, at present, they do not realise this. They are, in the main, themselves ruled by the cunning methods of the first class.
COUNT KORZYBSKI

In training a child to activity of thought, above all things we must beware of what I call 'inert ideas'—that is to say, ideas that are merely received into the mind without being utilised, or tested, or thrown into fresh combinations. In the history of education, the most striking phenomenon is that schools of learning, which at one epoch are alive with a ferment of genius, in a succeeding generation exhibit merely pedantry and routine. The reason is, that they are overladen with inert ideas. Education with inert ideas is not only useless; it is, above all things, harmful— *Corruptio optimi, pessima.* Except at rare intervals of intellectual ferment, education in the past has been radically infected with inert ideas. That is the reason why uneducated clever women, who have seen much of the world, are in middle life so much the most cultured part of the community. They have been saved from this horrible burden of inert ideas. Every intellectual revolution which has ever stirred humanity into greatness has been a passionate protest against inert ideas. Then, alas, with pathetic ignorance of human psychology, it has proceeded by some educational scheme to bind humanity afresh with inert ideas of its own fashioning.

Style, in its finest sense, is the last acquirement of the educated mind; it is also the most useful. It pervades the whole being. The administrator with a sense for style hates waste; the engineer with a sense for style economises his material; the artisan with a sense for style prefers good work. Style is the ultimate morality of mind.

A. N. WHITEHEAD : *The Aims of Education*

Discussions on education often assume that it is wholly beneficial. If only we can have more of it, society will be improved. The amount is what matters, not its contents or its objectives . . . that a rise in the general level of education will make society better, wiser and more adaptable to change. This would be true if our educational system were designed to make people better, wiser and more adaptable. But it is not so . . . Education is perhaps the most important problem in the world today; used aright it will make a better society; used wrongly it may destroy us.

GEORGE PICKERING : *The Challenge to Education*

WHILE IN NO DOUBT that criticism of our social system is amply justified, the author—as has already been made clear—shares the concern of those who see current protest as too often negative, limited, and lacking a coherent sense of direction.

Much of the blame for this must be laid at the doors of society's administrators, for it can hardly be questioned that today's educational ambitions show an over-narrow concern with instilling knowledge necessary for the economic rat-race and almost wholly neglect to equip the young to mould a society in which life could hold more meaning.

It is a disheartening fact that our present very proper

concern with the pollution of the land, oceans and the air is far from being balanced by an equal concern over the pollution of men's minds and values, for only such a blending of concerns can prove a mature awareness that true ecology demands both a biological and a sociological framework. But while we submit to the present excessively unbalanced State-controlled system of education, it is inevitable that concern with man's material well-being will be encouraged to obliterate any consideration of his spiritual and idealistic needs and ambitions.

It is hardly surprising that this lack of balance in our educational system has produced a generation in whom dissatisfaction is matched only by uncertainty as to how that dissatisfaction may be replaced by something more fulfilling. Only the exceptionally percipient have learned to isolate portions of their knowledge and to fit these together to create a pattern that at least partly satisfies their half-understood urge to contribute something more to the progress of society than they increasingly realise might more readily be supplied by a cog in a machine or a valve in a computer.

Thinking along these lines, are we not at the core of why this is an era of exceptional discontent and apprehension? For what are we doing by our present educational methods but spreading knowledge and at the same time trying to curb the awareness that wider knowledge inevitably brings? It is like force-feeding a goose in a shoe-box. That shoe-box, that only environment the goose knows, must in time split apart, but the goose-farmer has not recognised the need to provide a wider alternative home. Half, yet too rapidly, grown and without the security of a recognisable and habitable environment, the goose is ready only to flap into the first hazard that presents itself.

The State's vision of education is dominated by its blind determination to produce human automata for the perpetuation of an ever less meaningful and expanding status quo, and it has been all too successful in brainwashing parents into a condition of competitive concern to push, bully, bribe and plead their offspring into the mini rat-race for academic distinctions which not only fail to provide evidence of broad and balanced ability, but are increasingly being rejected as automatic passports to positions of greater power or profit. The sponge-like brain that can absorb and regurgitate facts may produce strings of A-levels and degrees, but as many teachers and personnel appointers can testify, such people all too often lack the common sense, the imagination and the initiative that in the long run go further and higher in creative and evolutionary terms than the computer-type brain.

It is enormously hopeful that these deficiencies in the present system are being recognised. There are definite signs that we are beginning to realise that to train children as a labour force for the needs of industry and science is not to educate them. Such thinking must in time begin to press for a reconstruction of educational ambitions—for a future in which educationists, instead of kow-towing to the requirements of commercial avarice and political ambition, begin to have a more positive say in the social and spiritual needs of those whom they are trying to educate. Properly, educationists should lead, not follow. This is obvious. That they do not is evidence only of their present powerlessness against State-determined economic priorities.

All of which adds up to the next overt fact, namely that it is our educationists, whether class-room teachers or Whitehall administrators, who above all have got to become better informed, better balanced, and in short just better people. In that we are all educationists of one kind or another, this boils down to the fact that every one of us must set his sights higher and not take refuge in a 'leave it to the schools' attitude—or at least not until the schools have thrown off their traditional and State-forged shackles and have returned to a better concept of what teaching really means.

For one of the worst aspects of the present situation is the loss of any realistic idealism, and this is strongly indicated by the tacit assumption that teachers have no ambitions beyond ensuring that they get better paid than bus conductors or dustmen. No one can reasonably deny that payment to the teaching profession should take account of what teachers' responsibilities are or should be, but what is so lamentable is that few concerned with the quality or quantity of teachers available seem willing to assume that tomorrow's school rooms might or should be staffed by young people with some degree of selflessness or responsibility beyond mere fact-pumping in the narrowest of contexts.

Yet teaching young minds is possibly the most important work any human being can perform, and there can be no more sad reflection on the present system than that student-teachers are as likely as not recruited from those who either lack ambition to go into anything else or have discovered that their talents are unlikely to command more supposedly glamorous or better-paid posts in other spheres. One is reminded of those more mature civilisations of the past wherein teachers and philosophers were accorded a status and degree of respect that we in the modern West show to few but pop singers, film stars, sportsmen and other trivia of the publicity machine.

'Well, you could always be a teacher, I suppose' is the kind of remark one has heard from the lips of parents who unsurprisingly have produced children who are as lacking as themselves in commitment or ambition for anything more than maximum rewards for minimum efforts. People might hesitate to say 'You could always be a lawyer' or 'an actor', or even 'a writer' or 'a painter', yet so undervalued and so superficially recognised is the enormously important task of true education that its administrators for the most part share the shallow and cynical view of all too many laymen. It is some comfort that many of those laymen have begun to lament the way society is going, though all too often without realising the link between education, values and behaviour. Man's inability to see the connection between cause and effect is often breath-depriving, but never more so than in this context.

If those young people who might become teachers are never told and convinced that teaching is work of such tremendous importance and responsibility, but only that if they do it they will be unappreciated and under-paid, what quality of mind is going to be attracted into the profession? On a purely practical level, what is urgently needed is a teacher recruiting policy that relies in the main not upon material incentives but upon appealing to that desire 'to contribute' and for personal fulfilment that lies in the hearts of most young people, but must inevitably be coarsened and dulled by the continual propaganda of avaricious agitators who can see no point in anything beyond instant material rewards.

The need for good and dedicated teachers is the greatest need of the world today, save only perhaps for a vast reduction in the spread of our species (and this is something that will only come through proper education in the priorities). Sadly, many of today's teachers are not of such quality that they can claim to be performing significantly more useful functions than those envied bus conductors and dustmen, but this is a negative observation and does not exclude the necessity to change that state of affairs at the earliest opportunity and in the most realistic manner. The change can only come about by convincing the administrators and recruiters of our educators of the need to set higher standards and ambitions. Until the right lead is given, the quality of applicants must inevitably be low.

All argument along these lines leads to the same conclusion—that our values and aims need to be re-thought; that mankind has a greater potential than the mere achievement of a more satisfactory GNP; that it is actually possible to combine material day-to-day existence with an ethical code and so live more fully and more meaningfully.

To some, all such argument is mere pie-in-the-sky idealism, totally out of touch with present-day 'realities'. There are, indeed, men and women whose only goal in life is a larger car or a newer washing machine. They will not be reading this book. They are satisfied, for the present, by a workshop manual and the colour supplements' advertisements.

But there is a more important section that accepts the necessity that is being argued but cannot see how it can be realised. They should not mis-read as cold comfort the assurance that their mere existence is what matters, at this stage, above all else.

For the destiny of mankind has never been decided by instant answers. All true growth is a painfully slow process, brought about not by over-night sensational purges, pogroms and 'liberations', but by the accumulated realisations and efforts of a significant minority of men and women who have developed their awareness to the point where they can grasp at least a grain of the truth that mankind needs to see and accept wholly if we are to realise our potential.

Most mature teachers would accept this very evident fact. What it is less easy for most of us to do is to remain aware of the continuation of that process. It is extremely easy to become almost cripplingly depressed by the apparent unchangeability of society's values. And this is precisely why the best teachers are those who are not only aware of the need for growth in ideas and ambitions, but also of the evolutionary fact that, whatever the day-to-day evidence to the contrary may suggest, the very existence and nurturing of a properly-based dissatisfaction must, however slowly, alter the course of events and lift society as a whole on to a new dimension of consciousness.

If teachers with this vision are also aware that in any reconstruction of educational ambitions there must be many behavioural patterns needing radical overhaul if future generations are to build a society guided by a consistent and realistic morality rather than by the political and commercial pressures of a degenerate Establishment, then they have it within their sphere of influence to make the major contribution towards building a world that could at last merit the term 'civilisation'.

So in this chapter more than in any other it has to be emphasised that 'protest' needs to be directed at the *total* human condition—at the spiritual state of 'deplorably unimproved man'. Society needs to feel anger with itself, not just with its scapegoats. It is for the teachers of every new generation to realise and experience their responsibilities in helping in so vital a manner to mould the shape and purpose of the future. In order to do this, they simply have no choice but to understand and promote what might best be termed the Civilised Alternative. If mankind is to survive its own cleverness, that Alternative demands cultivation of eclecticism and of a far more broadly based rejection of violence. These are the twin foundation stones without which no new educational structure can do more than preserve the status quo for a little longer. With proper foundations, the solution to over-population, wars, pollution and the rest of it depends only upon enlightened administration, for the goodwill went into the footings. The enlightenment must grow in proportion to our growth in eclecticism. It cannot do otherwise.

Just how, by what means and machinery, by what precise methods of persuasion and influence, new concepts and aims may infiltrate men's minds, aims and institutions, is beyond the present brief. With the foundations laid, the form of the superstructure will become evident. When conviction and purpose are strong enough, means are invariably found. What matters is the strength of the conviction, the certainty of the purpose. Above all, what is needed are people, individuals, who respond to this reasoning positively rather than negatively. Progress is ensured by those who say 'I can and I will'. The status quo is maintained by the 'realists' who say 'I can't and I won't'. Our main hope today lies in the fact that even the most orthodox and head-in-the-sand establishmentarians are beginning to realise that there is no longer any such beast as the status quo or, at best, that it is a pretty sick animal that has got to be replaced.

Whatever the ideology or brief, with conviction and purpose assured, the means and rapidity of the communication are bound to be realised. Any teacher, faced by a class-room full of children from home backgrounds where probably the greatest indoctrination has come from commercial television and the negative restraints of parents who have neither time nor inclination to see their children as creatures of varying potential and needs, has in his or her hands powers that should humble as much as they should inspire. It is a terrible reflection on the state of our society that at present nine out of ten teachers are encouraged, directly and by omission, to regard such a classroom as nothing but a challenge to maintain order and get examination results. By many it is seen as little but an uncomfortable way of earning an inadequate wage packet, or as something to do before marriage.

But, again to underline the what-should-be-obvious, nothing can be done about that state of society until enough of us see it clearly and are determined to change it. Nor is it any good hoping to change society until we have changed ourselves, for society consists only of people and can do no better than those people. Society does not enjoy a separate, isolated state of being with values and aims higher than the individuals who make it up. Society is us. We are society. When we put our own house in order we improve society by precisely that amount—perhaps by rather more than that if we take into account the infectious quality of example.

This was more obvious to thinking people a hundred years ago than it is today. Today we look hopefully, if in vain, to our technology to save us from our personal deficiencies. But what we have not sufficiently woken up to as yet is that while doing away with the ritual and dogma of organised religion we also deprived ourselves of the essential discipline—and, consequently, comfort—of those moral guide-lines that have lain hidden, like veins and arteries, in the all too fleshly body of the established church. The cholesterol level in the bloodstream of that life-giving network may have been dangerously high, but while the tired heart was capable of action it produced at least a few red corpuscles to supply that ethical oxygen without which life must lose its meaning.

The old discipline having been thrown away with the obsolete trappings of sectarian religion, it is vital that we should develop a substitute morality within the framework of formal and acquired education. The best that lay in religious belief must be preserved and expanded as a separate discipline, no less in the home than in schools and universities. It must be seen as a greater priority than education in artistic appreciation, political awareness, sex, or even the three 'Rs' and the cerebral abstractions of what passes for philosophy at the more advanced levels of academic education. The empiricism of logical positivism, with its naïve respect for the power of modern science, is no substitute for a positive morality concerned with the first principles of human conduct and responsibility. The term 'philosophy' has been debased to cover a multitude of sins (not least of omission), whereas its original purpose was to clarify a handful of essential virtues. Pedantry has turned philosophy into a dead-end specialism at a time when the world has a crying need for an activating principle that only true philosophy can competently serve.

At heart most men and women wish to set their sights on something higher. 'Higher' may not necessarily mean 'better' and all too often is a quantitative rather than a qualitative term. But the kernel of truth remains—that however despairingly one may compare the actions of humans with those of lower beings, man's most distinguishing feature is his ability to stand outside his appetites and failings and accept the necessity for moral and social improvement. If we do not believe that men possess this urge to be better, then we might as well swallow the pill to end all pills as a practical means of promoting the idea of racial extinction as the only answer to our predicament. It would be the only logical thing to do.

Few, if any, of the facts and arguments in this book are new. But their correlation points, as does the current dissatisfaction among the young, to the possibility of so radical a change in mankind's behavioural and visionary pattern that to that degree this study may make its small contribution to a phase in man's brief history which only his short-sightedness and slavery to habit and tradition is preventing him from experiencing.

TEN

Progress out of Protest

What could begin to deny self, if there were not something in man different from self?

WILLIAM LAW

Two things fill the mind with ever new and increasing awe: the stars above me and the moral law within me.

IMMANUEL KANT

THE BULK OF THIS BOOK has necessarily been concerned with the main faults in our society and with how these faults may be met by a reorientation of personal aims and educational responsibilities. It may be apparent how acceptance of this alternative viewpoint must affect the course and form of the life-style of the so-called civilised world, though it should not be supposed that so brief a study is claiming to have presented the complete answer to the problems of mankind! Such pinnacled omniscience is beyond the grasp of any one book or person, and even the greatest philosophers have not been wholly free from sectionalism.

But some signposts are clearly marked and are rooted in assessable facts. One of the most important of these is that at this stage in history Euro-American culture dominates the international scene. Being a grossly materialistic culture, prompted by the profit motive although often claiming an altruistic concern to help emergent nations to establish viable economies, it has so far squandered its influence by the exportation of goods, values and habits that have ensured a rapid corruption of the host countries so easily dazzled by the gewgaws of the West.

For our exported culture has been dominated by our militarism, our dehumanising industrial and agrarian technologies, our devitalised foodstuffs and carnivorous obsessions, our irresponsible chemical and scientific tampering, and most aspects of that sick and violent life-style—embodied all too depressingly in much of our art and literature—by which we have fondly imagined we could control and improve the natural world.

Those who have questioned the desirability of exporting such a way of life have been sharply reminded of the material benefits to the recipients, but are we now in any position to assert that in the long term those benefits will have outweighed the disadvantages? We have only to note where our own society is going to see the answer. To equate washing machines, motor cars or even such apparent blessings as increased longevity and land reclamation with beneficial progress in the evolutionary sense, is proof of little but our naïve materialism.

But this is again to assert the negative viewpoint. The positive one is that we must recognise our future responsibilities not only to ourselves but also to those countries and nations that rely upon the West for much of their cultural and economic growth. If our lead is wrong, then we take the whole world with us over the brink. If it is right, then a world-pattern must in time be established that will be sound in its foundations and consistent in its aims. If this seems an impossible dream, then our scepticism is evidence only of the depth of our despair over the world we have made for ourselves. But despair—or, at least, acute dissatisfaction—was ever the prerequisite for reform.

At best, however, we are still talking of A.D. Somewhen. It cannot be otherwise. It has taken a good deal of time to get ourselves into the present mess, and no two-day sit-down or bloody revolution is going to alter the situation. Only the relatively slow process of a change in sentiment is going to have any lasting effect. That change will have to be seen, to a lesser or greater extent, in almost every aspect of our lives. But we shall be willing to accept this as soon as we have accepted the necessity and the possibility, for it must be built into the new educational framework.

The needed pattern is not difficult to conceive. What is more of a problem is the overcoming of our impatience for over-night remedies. But the solutions are long term, the palliatives short term. We must *now*, before the eleventh hour is past, create the basis and the structural skeleton for the long-term solutions. This can only be done when we stop deceiving ourselves that continual patching of the existing framework's rotten fabric is going to avert disaster. The fabric is decaying and the framework is obsolete. With the tools and the knowledge now available to us, we must build from new foundations. There is no other answer.

It is time to summarise. In these glimpses of the Civilised Alternative, what kind of society is being visualised? First and foremost, on a personal level it must involve the kind of individual reassessment that has already been outlined as vital to true progress, demanding the cultivation of an eclectic outlook that must inevitably lead to behavioural changes that are consistent with a compassionate (= civilised) alternative to the present basically violent, avaricious and sectional way of life. This personal reorientation is absolutely vital. A consistent life must give hope of a consistent society. Nothing will be achieved if, disliking the demands it would make upon us, we ignore the essential disciplines and look once more to the external, imposed, delegated, organisational and governmental answers that never have been and, in their present form, never will be answers at all.

Given that realisation and its application, then on an institutional level much research will be necessary into the effects of organisations on their individual components and on the original credo or desidero that brought the structure into being. In many instances it will almost certainly be seen that organisations must be scaled down in size and in other respects subjected to a humanising process that will ensure supervision of their functions and structure and will keep alive the corporate awareness of the underlying terms of reference.

On the scientific side it is encouraging that already much is being written and discussed that proves that even some of the most orthodox observers are having serious doubts about the application in both military and civilian spheres of the advice of scientists working for governments. Some scientists are themselves experiencing breakthroughs of conscience that would have been unheard of, or at least unreported, a few years ago. In a speech to the Royal Institution, one professor of biology, concerned by the ill-considered and dangerous application of scientific advice, recently challenged the myth that although the uses society makes of science may be good or evil, the scientist has no special responsibility for those uses save as a normal citizen.

This myth, he emphasised, has sprung from the view of science as the pursuit of natural laws which are valid irrespective of the nation, race, politics, religion or class of the discoverer. The technological imperative states that whatever it is possible to conceive of being done by science and technology must and will be done, whether for exploration or consolidation, for creation or destruction. But this anarchistic philosophy of developmental inevitability makes the dedicated scientist subservient to the technology of his own creation. The notion that scientific developments are unforeseeable and unplanned is to whitewash the many consequential abuses of that development as being themselves unplanned and accidental, whereas it should be—and now is being—seen that the vast bulk of scientific research by the major powers comes under the heading of science conceived for specific and deliberate ends.

That greed and violence is the driving force behind so much of this research has already been stressed, and it goes without saying that in a society prompted, through a better concept of education, by different motives, science can become a tool to serve a more mature and responsible vision of what is for the good of mankind and the world they inhabit.

On the related economic level there has clearly got to be a vast change in current sentiments. In their nurturing of outworn concepts all too many economists make Colonel Blimp look like an up-to-the-minute symbol of progressive thought. Challenged to justify their far too common defence of an uncontrolled upward spiral of population, economists may often be heard speaking of the GNP in tones of deep secular reverence, and it seems hardly to have dawned on some of them that such phenomena as automation and computerisation have for long been pointing to the paramount necessity to change our attitude to the excess of our species from one of quantitative self-congratulation to a profound qualitative concern. Blindfolded handmaidens of a politically dominated consumer society, economists show few signs of producing spokesmen qualified and prepared to point out that the present industrial-scientific complex, totally committed to such suicidal idiocies as a vast worldwide armaments race and planned obsolescence (already an anachronism in a polluted and over-peopled world whose natural resources are rapidly being exhausted), must experience a total about-face that will in fact evolve naturally in a society wherein more benign personal and educational influences have been given room and time to work.

On a national level, each country's main responsibility will be to lay the proper educational foundations for the creation of a society that will think and feel and act eclectically and compassionately, and with mature ecological awareness, which is to say internationally. The 'Common Market' must embrace the whole world, not merely a handful of European nations concerned with maintaining a higher standard of material living than the rest.

Which brings us to the obvious and undeniable fact that little can be done in corporate terms until, on an international level, we can co-operate in the creation of a form of World Government to agree upon and supervise those matters that are of common concern. Such a supra-government must clearly devote itself to such monumentally important issues as a world population policy; an international police force to replace national militarism; the control, reduction and eventual abolition of armaments; the basics of a new world-wide educational system; and an international economic pattern that will have nothing to do with capitalism, communism, socialism or any other ism or ology, for it will be above all political affiliations in the totality and equitableness of its concern.

Before the charge of hopeless idealism is thrown at this very condensed suggestion of how our society might look in years to come, let us consider that nothing has been suggested that could conceivably be said to be impossible and beyond man's intelligence to implement. Indeed, such ideas are for the most part nothing new. What has been lacking until now has been the awareness of the need for so fundamental a reorientation of mankind's purpose and values. Without that awareness, prompted by fear of the consequences of his own folly, man has been unwilling to submit to a change in sentiment and so to a change in the structure of international society. Today we have both the intelligence and the equipment (particularly in the field of communications) to turn the shelved dreams of the past into actuality. All through history moments have come in the affairs of men when radical change and reappraisement is the only next step that can be taken. We have reached such a moment now—and the biggest of them all. The precise methods to be employed are not within the compass of this book—they will begin to become clear as soon as the required machinery is set in motion. That machinery is under the control of anyone who can see what education should really be about and who fears for the future of a society in danger of being controlled by clever devils rather than by wise men.

'Hell,' said Sartre with some prescience in *Huis Clos,* 'is other people,' and a factor that may seem to have been under-emphasised in this book is the contribution that over-population and physical pollution have made to world problems. Any lack of emphasis on such enormously important matters is due not to the author's indifference but to the heartening fact that massive attention is already being given to the statistics and implications of these problems, and it is not within the scope of this book to present an undue proportion of known and widely discussed facts.

But, certainly, it is only possible to visualise a more rational and humane society conducted on the lines that have been suggested if we can also imagine a future world in which the human population is dramatically less than it is today. Here, again, it is necessary to take the long-term view. It is always hard for some of us to do this, but there can be no reasonable doubt that if man is to survive as man and not as some form of remote-controlled termite existing in the vertical layers of a vast ant-heap, then the day must come when he has so reduced and controlled his numbers that he has at last proved the strength of his concern to achieve true ecological balance. What the future optimum world population figure for homo sapiens may be it is impossible to say at this time when we can indeed not see the wood for the trees. It may be 1,000 million or 100 million; it may even be only 10 million. It is fruitless to conjecture.

So much depends on whether our future values are governed by quantitative or qualitative considerations. All we need accept for the present is that it must be reduced and that the process must begin now. Reduction or destruction—we know now that this is the choice, and for most of us the prospect of the former is presumably more acceptable than the latter. But the choice must be made, consciously and without further delay. The ranks of the prophets of doom contain too many and too distinguished men and women for their perceptions any longer to be dismissed as the Jonah-like exaggerations of a handful of cranks. For the young, at any rate, the short term appeal of the profits *from* doom have begun to have a very hollow sound.

Few thinking people, even today, are so severed from the roots of a more balanced social condition that they cannot visualise the relatively early return of a world in which our numbers will be so reduced that the resources (even if no longer 'natural' in the sense of being the primary basics of iron, coal, oil, etc.) will be enough for all; in which an unpolluted environment, pure food, space and a proper balance between work and leisure—or at least a tolerable approximation to this improved society—are taken for granted as our natural birthright; in which a better and fuller sense of education has replaced our avaricious and violent ambitions by a more satisfying sense of purpose and responsibility; in which spreading urbanisation, traffic congestion and a hundred and one other problems of excessive population have been eliminated; in which technology, under the control of men and women with more mature values, serves need instead of creating and intensifying boredom by making empty lives emptier and idle hands more idle.

Utopian? Not really. But, in any case, only the simple can be horrified by the theoretical sterility of Utopia.

Perhaps the only negative doom-thought in this whole argument is that man will never so conquer himself and his problems that he can afford to sit back and bask in the knowledge that there is nothing more to be achieved. He will never, on this planet or any other, achieve Utopia, if for no other reason than that he would hate it if he did.

Desire, it has been said, is prayer, and this may suggest to those with orthodox sectarian convictions some new or expanded paths to explore. One hopes so. The purpose of this book is most certainly not to destroy or exclude faith, but to expand its boundaries, to eliminate its restrictions, and to make sense to a generation impatient with the limitations of orthodoxies, organisations and specialisms. Nor is it being suggested that, in the long term, the answer lies in eclecticism for the few. The best results must come from the practice of eclecticism by every person capable of being educated and of seeing the fundamental values on which our education must be founded. The pursuit of the whole, by the many, for us all—the direct opposite of our present ill: the pursuit of the selective, by the few, for themselves.

Those who may say the goals outlined in this book are unattainable are ignoring first principles. Nature herself observes and encourages balance. The kind of society we can and must create would be a more balanced society. It would not, for instance, be so hopelessly and illogically divided in its attitude towards violence. An over-crowded society that breeds the tensions and greeds that create the problems of war, cruelty to children and animals, poverty and pollution, must look like a lunatic asylum to any impartial observer who witnesses the lip-service we pay to peace movements, kindness to weaker creatures, social welfare and the conservation of our environment.

It follows that perhaps the only unanswerable critic of this way of thinking will be the man or woman who says: 'I like this world as it is. I do not object to the violence and cruelty and greed, for I am adjusted to it and am prepared to take my chance with the rest. I am out for myself. I hate or am indifferent to my neighbour unless I can get something out of him. Idealism and social discontent are strictly for the maladjusted. I am a balanced and uncomplaining individual who, helped by science and technology, may somehow survive the dangers of our era, or at worst go down fighting without regret or remorse and in the belief that the generations to follow must solve their problems for themselves.' Such anti-philosophers will not have got further than the blurb on the dust-jacket. But one thing is certain, and this is that anyone who reads this book and responds favourably to no more than a part of it, is proof that there is hope for the future. For as has been suggested, the one fact that entitles man to claim any superiority over other animals is that he alone is capable of questioning and disliking and outgrowing his so-called instincts and patterns of behaviour. It is the most hopeful fact in the evolution of the human species, for if we are not all slaves of our instincts we are potentially masters of our souls and

—as far as we can visualise it—of our destiny. This is the most important realisation of all, but it has to be examined not within the context of the scientific, technocratic, sectarian or specialist ambition, but in the light of our now overriding necessity to develop and be guided by the principles and practice of a compassionate eclecticism. With calculated repetitiveness it must be said again that reorganisation and rationalisation do not lie in the hands of organisations and factions, however worthy their declared aims may be, but rather in the minds and convictions and determination of every individual. You, me and the next man.

But it is impossible to predict with any confidence about the exact nature of the very distant future. Maybe the swing of humanity's colossal pendulum will one day bring us back to some form of Arcadia wherein we discover the root values of life as nature may have intended it for our species. To all but those who have been totally corrupted by urban/technological values there is something extremely sane in the ambitions of that school of thinking represented by Voltaire, Thoreau, Rousseau, Swedenborg, Kant, Schopenhauer, Alcott, Tolstoy and many others who have seen at least part of the desirable alternative. But we cannot reverse the clock to recapture time past. We can only set it for time to come. For the future over which we of the present era have some control, one can predict only the absolute necessity for the beginning of a de-escalation and reorientation—a de-escalation of populations with all the reduction in both physical and mental pollutional damage that this must help to bring about, and a reorientation of values that will in time turn science and technology into a beneficent tool instead of a monstrous tyranny.

But this is not the issue here and now. What we are discussing is survival in any meaningful sense of that word —how best and least destructively to survive in a world that is rapidly getting out of hand due to mankind's greed, violence and short-sightedness. We must leave the problems of Utopia, or its approximation, to later generations. Our problem, apart from immediate survival, is to ensure that those later generations exist and are in a fit condition to think their way into any sort of future worth having. Unless we can put our own twentieth-century house in order, the future of mankind will be the same as that enjoyed by the dodo and a lot of other species since, and while some of us may have moments of feeling that such a solution is not without its merits, the present writer is assuming that in most of us there is still some small spark of evolutionary ambition, some vague inkling that for all his faults man might conceivably be destined for (or, if you prefer, just capable of) something more contributory to universal progress than self-extinction in his present half-human form. And surely we are intelligent enough to avoid that fate? Already one blueprint for survival, supported by many and eminent scientists and conservationists, has emphasised the necessity for decentralisation and de-urbanisation and a return to village communities, village politics and village industries. This is a welcome breakthrough, but any realistic blueprint must embrace more than industrial and economic reappraisal or the merely physical facts of ecology. Mankind cannot survive unless we also accept the inescapable need for a moral code, independent of any particular theology, that is capable of acceptance as a common standard for all humanity.

As we watch film of the latest box of tricks being pumped up to the moon or beyond, shedding on route its allotted quota of gash metal or other pollution into perpetual orbit, we may wonder at the technical achievement that lies behind the demonstration. But our stronger sensation may well be one of sadness that so much thought and endeavour should have been employed to such a pointless end in a world on whose list of priorities moon excursions should surely come a long way down. The monkey mind, unfortunately, finds it easier and more exciting to ship its unresolved problems to other planets than to tackle the really tough and demanding issues on earth. And this is the great danger—that our technology increasingly encourages us to focus our attention on the escape hatch instead of on perfecting the working of the system by which we have to progress.

Many, as has been said, will not find it difficult, reasoning from their own premises, to tear the preceding arguments into shreds; to make formidable lists of the barriers—physical, cultural, economic, social and mental—that lie between sight of the goal and its realisation; to question man's ability to reorientate his thoughts and ambitions; to assert his innate violence and greed; to reaffirm that because we are now on the bandwagon of science and technology, ergo science and technology can and must solve all our problems. But to all sceptics and critics and pessimists the answer must be what it has always been, namely that nothing is lost or hopeless unless we are determined to defy the rules of cause and effect and to deny the possibility of our futures being influenced by something lying beyond the patent limitations of the materialistic hypothesis.

There was a lot to be said for the primitive methods of days gone by when we frightened and encouraged ourselves with clear-cut visions of what was 'good' or 'evil'. Life became a lot more complicated when Freud took over from God, for while spokesmen of the latter have talked as much drivel as interpreters of the former, at least you knew (or thought you knew) where you stood with God. Bogy or father-figure, he ran a very efficient sorting office. Either you conformed or you were for the high-jump. But today we are governed not by a God-imposed morality but by a man-justified expediency, and if we are to survive the latter we must also have some degree of, or substitute for, the former. And that, perhaps, is what these submissions are all about—the need and framework for a sense of purpose.

Right at the beginning it was emphasised that this was not a religious book in any sectarian sense of that word. It has attempted, nevertheless, to recognise that we all, young or old, deeply and unavoidably need a sense of direction—or at least guidelines, even if we do not know what, if anything, lies on the other side of that labyrinth we call life. For some, organised religion has at least provided a kind of discipline, even though it has as a rule overstrained credibility in matters of dogma and destination. Today the old symbols are largely out-moded. In an increasingly sophisticated society this was inevitable. Nor does it matter so long as we realise that it is man's supreme folly and arrogance to imagine that he can live in balance, harmony and happiness without self-discipline; without a sense of purpose beyond mere material acquisition; without concern to make an evolutionary contribution to the world we go on sharing only if we abide by certain rules that are common and vital to our species; without, in short, seeing our place in nature as a small but subtly significant microcosm within the macrocosm.

We have all the knowledge we need to build those new values, that new society, that wise-more-than-brave new world that is the only alternative to rapid descent into a violent, rapacious, technology-dominated jungle and the final obliteration of everything that deserves the label of 'human'. The problems of achieving that world can be solved only when, *individually*, we accept and act upon our personal responsibility to contribute to its creation. This book has sought to suggest where the immediate priorities lie; which habits and sentiments need rethinking; in short, what kind of basis must be provided for the future if man is to survive the consequences of failing to lay the corner stones of wisdom to support the painted paper walls of his mere cleverness.

Now, as at any time in history, the future lies in the hands of individual men and women. Not, in the final analysis, in organisations, machines, economies, politics, wars, strikes, revolutions, religions, philosophies, art, or even literature. All these may reflect, stimulate or pervert the social trends and mores, but it cannot be too often repeated and remembered that none exists or has lasting power without the day-to-day support, enthusiasm and abilities of the individuals who create, sustain, modify or reject them according to the quality and preoccupations of their minds. We have all been so brain-washed into the belief that answers must be political and organisational that the notion of a racial-rescue programme centred on individual self-improvement has become overlaid by fears and reservations that are more the product of our over-sophisticated and confused minds than proof of a fundamentally irremediable situation. We tend to prefer our panaceas and philosophies to be wordy, complicated, abstruse, and therefore susceptible to innumerable interpretations that lead to argument rather than to action. A full hand of questionable interpretations is less demanding, more easily side-stepped, than that steely 'still small voice' that tells us there is only one fundamental answer and that it lies within each one of us. Like pedantic scholars, we feel more at home wandering and quarrelling among the footnotes than in living out the basic argument of the thesis. The fact remains that the only way to change the system is to become the system. Hence the vital importance of realising that the chief need is to concentrate on the form of our individual 'becoming'. There is absolutely no organisational or group substitute for this most basic of basics.

All of which is to repeat that the future will be determined by the quality of our education; by the values which, as individuals, we formulate and pass on, whether we be parents, teachers, or just people meeting people in the course of our social and business lives. It is a responsibility and a challenge that, properly understood, should be big enough to prevent any of us from feeling a lack of direction or purpose. Inevitably, out of the pattern of our protest will evolve awareness of the means to, and a progressively clearer vision of, the objective. Hence the inestimable importance of agreeing on the nature of that pattern—a problem that is no bigger than our individual disinclinations to solve it.

FURTHER READING

The aim of this short bibliography is to suggest some key works, mostly of general interest, in the main areas discussed in this book. The bibliographies in several of the works listed will usefully extend the available reading. Dates shown are not necessarily of the first editions, preference being given to paperback or cheap editions, or to the latest known reissue.

Barr, John (Editor): *The Environmental Handbook.* Ballantine/Pan, 1971

Bergson, Henri: *Creative Evolution.* Macmillan, 1965

Carrel, A.: *Man, the Unknown.* Burns Oates, 1961

Carson, Rachel: *Silent Spring.* Hamish Hamilton, 1963

Commoner, Barry: *Science and Survival.* Gollancz, 1966

du Noüy, Lecomte: *Human Destiny.* Longmans/Mentor, 1958

Ehrlich, Paul R.: *The Population Bomb.* Ballantine/Pan, 1971

Ellul, Jacques: *Violence.* SCM Press, 1970

Fabre-Luce, Alfred: *Men or Insects?* Hutchinson, 1964

Hardy, Alister: *The Living Stream.* Collins, 1965

Harrison, R.: *Animal Machines.* Vincent Stuart, 1964

Huxley, Aldous: *Brave New World.* Chatto & Windus, 1950

———: *Ends and Means*. Chatto & Windus, 1966
———: *The Perennial Philosophy*. Fontana, 1958
James, William: *The Varieties of Religious Experience*. Fontana, 1960
Jung, C. G.: *Modern Man in Search of a Soul*. Routledge, 1947
Le Bon, Gustave: *The Crowd*. Viking, 1960
Lorenz, Konrad: *On Aggression*. Methuen, 1966
Muller, Herbert J.: *The Uses of the Past*. O.U.P., 1952
Mumford, Lewis: *The Pentagon of Power*. Secker & Warburg, 1971
Orwell, George: *Animal Farm*. Longmans, 1965
———: *Nineteen Eighty-Four*. Heinemann, 1965
Packard, Vance: *The Hidden Persuaders*. Penguin, 1963
———: *The Waste Makers*. Penguin, 1963
Pappworth, M. H.: *Human Guinea Pigs*. Routledge, 1967
Pine, L. G.: *After Their Blood*. Kimber, 1966
Rudd, Geoffrey L.: *Why Kill for Food?* The Vegetarian Society, 1956
Stevens, Henry Bailey: *The Recovery of Culture*. Harper, 1953
Storr, Anthony: *Human Aggression*. Penguin, 1970
Taylor, Gordon Rattray: *The Doomsday Book*. Thames & Hudson, 1970
Tolstoy, Leo: *Essays and Letters*. O.U.P., 1925
Trotter, W.: *Instincts of the Herd in Peace and War*. O.U.P., 1953

Turner, E. S.: *All Heaven in a Rage*. Michael Joseph, 1964

Vyvyan, John: *The Dark Face of Science*. Michael Joseph, 1971

Walker, Roy: *The Golden Feast*. Rockliff, 1952

Whitehead, A. N.: *The Aims of Education*. Benn, 1962

Williams, Duncan: *Trousered Apes*. Churchill Press, 1971

Williams, Howard: *The Ethics of Diet*. Broadbent, 1907

Wynne-Edwards, V. C.: *Animal Dispersion in Relation to Social Behaviour*. Oliver & Boyd, 1962

Index

Index

Index

Index